Synergistic Rhythm

Synergistic Rhythm
Building A Thriving, Profitable Business

Edward C. Garner, Jr.

Published by Game Changer Publishing

Paperback ISBN: 978-1-962656-53-5
Hardcover ISBN: 978-1-962656-54-2
Digital: ISBN: 978-1-962656-55-9

www.GameChangerPublishing.com

DEDICATION

My heart overflows with deep gratitude to my beloved wife, Patty, of 36 years! I honor her ability to love unconditionally, forgive quickly, and her extraordinary capacity to celebrate! I am thankful for her thoughtful ways of extending grace, to care with compassion, to encourage and understand the bigger picture of life. I am grateful for having Patty walk beside me and being my personal partner in life and business. The way she loves and her heart for others to make a difference is truly astonishing! She is an amazing gift to me and our family!

I also acknowledge our three married children and their spouses, Matthew and Tori, Michael and Katie, and Merv and Andrea. Their love and support over the years have been precious to me in so many ways. Their hearts to see lives transformed is so beautiful, and each one of them is an exceptional leader in raising up world-changing children. They have all influenced my life in bountiful ways. We are currently blessed with six grandchildren.

My gratitude and honor to God, who has met me in my weakest moments, transformed my life, and strengthened me to get up, keep going, and go encourage another life! I am so grateful for God's loving grace. My favorite book that inspires me daily is the Bible.

Truforth Team, thank you for your remarkable support, cheerleading, coaching, and creative brilliance. I am forever grateful for your inspiration, your dares, your dreams, your feedback, and the way you love big and extend grace for our pace. I am forever grateful! Thank you for your hearts for transformation.

To all the coaches, clients, mentors, pastors, friends, family, and church family who have encouraged me with insights, inspiration, and encouragement. Thanks for your love, kindness, words of affirmation, and for empowering my life and family. You influence my life in bountiful ways to get out of my comfort zone, stretch, grow, and ignite, train, and transform lives. I am forever grateful for you in my life!

A special thank you to my coach and facilitation mentor, Janet, who saw the gift in me and worked with me to develop the coaching and facilitation gift. Thank you for all the years of training and learning from you! Thank you for believing in me!

In honor of the Amish family, I had the greatest privilege of working on their farm for almost a decade while growing up, learning countless life and entrepreneurial skills that formed values in my life. You impacted my life with a love for family, the outdoors, animals, and seeing things grow. I loved serving your family. Thank you for all you taught me and poured into me. You have impacted my life and shaped who I was becoming during those formative years, and I am forever grateful.

I want to honor my grandparents, George and Theresa, for always believing in me and teaching me many principles of life. They have always created a loving, safe place for me, and I loved spending time exploring their property and being with them.

I am grateful for my sister Charlotte, who has always had a special place in my heart. She and I walked through a lot growing up. She has always been there and is a rare and precious gift to my life.

I honor my mom for her love, always believing in me, for the thousand and one things she has done for my life and family growing up. My mom had a way of making things work out from whatever was available. Mom, you marked my life with your heart, care, and thoughtfulness, protecting us many times from many situations. I owe you my life, Mom! I honor my mom's husband, Ed, of 30-plus years. You have been a stable pillar of strength and love for her, and it has meant so much to me to see her cared for and loved through all these years and how you have given her a new life!

I honor my Dad for teaching me many life skills, such as carpentry, building homes, and renovating buildings. My Dad was always someone I could call and process life with. My Dad and I had a very tumultuous relationship for 25 years. Then, both of our lives changed when we met Jesus, and my Dad became one of my best friends. My Dad had a way of working around difficult situations like a specialist. He was a talented entrepreneur and taught me many business strategies. He had the biggest heart to help so many lives through their addictions. My Dad's life was transformed, and he helped many people find freedom from addictions. I am forever grateful and miss him so much.

To all the leaders who read this book, allow me to take a moment and share my deepest gratitude! My heart is that your flame would be ignited to go out and ignite many other candles to make the world a brighter and better place!

I'd like to thank Game Changer Publisher for the great delight of working with Alex and Cris and their team! I am so grateful for all their insights, coaching, and excellence in making this book come alive!

Read This First

We sincerely appreciate your purchase and the time you've dedicated to reading my book. To express our gratitude, we're thrilled to offer you a collection of complimentary resources! Our ultimate goal is to empower and inspire you to discover your own unique rhythm, not only through the pages of this book but also with the extra materials we're delighted to share with you, absolutely free of charge.

Scan the QR Code Here:

Synergistic Rhythm

Building A Thriving, Profitable Business

Edward C. Garner, Jr.

www.GameChangerPublishing.com

Foreword

Dear Reader,

Welcome to the dynamic world of coaching, where the paths of professionals intersect, and genuine connections unfold. It is my pleasure to introduce you to Ed Garner, a man dedicated to empowering those seeking to elevate their business and leadership skills—the insightful mind behind this book and someone I am honored to call my friend.

Hosting Ed on my podcast was inspiring, and within the first few minutes of our conversation, the warmth of his encouragement and the sincerity of his desire to uplift individuals was clear. It was in those initial moments that I knew I had made a friend for life.

As a seasoned Certified Master and Business Coach, Ed leverages decades of experience working within organizations and as a trusted coach to simplify the myriad of tasks leaders encounter. In a world often marked by professional distances, Ed stands out as a beacon of authentic support, embodying the true spirit of coaching.

Whether you are a new business owner, entrepreneur, solopreneur, small business owner, a seasoned professional, or contemplating the journey of starting your own business, this book is tailored specifically for you.

Ed's desire to foster hope and inspire readers to connect through core values, all while embracing the ebb and flow of an organization's daily challenges, is the essence of "Synergistic Rhythm." This book doesn't rely on theories but is a reservoir of hard-earned experience, embodying the journey of a man who has experienced it all and is enthusiastic about sharing insights that genuinely matter, both personally and professionally. As you explore the pages and wisdom of "Synergistic Rhythm," let these insights illuminate your path. Ed's commitment to nurturing growth and resilience isn't just theoretical; it's a tangible reality that brings authenticity to the principles and core values he imparts.

May the pages of this book inspire you, as they have inspired me, with the unwavering encouragement and genuine connection that defines Ed Garner's coaching philosophy. Remember, as Ed always says, "You've got what it takes!"

Dominica Lumazar
Certified Executive & Business Coach
#1 International Bestselling Author

Table of Contents

Introduction

Why Synergistic Rhythm? Have you ever seen a dance team that had an effervescent, harmonious rhythm that drew you in and captivated you? Maybe you have watched a choreographed marching band and heard their vibrant sounds that seemed magnetic. We know rhythm is actually essential to the quality of life. Allow me to shine a light on just how vital rhythm is for you as a leader.

I can remember finishing up a meeting in our local town, and the sounds of a marching band echoed uniquely throughout the streets. The beat of the drums and instruments drew us up the street to be mesmerized by their rhythm and sound. We were so captivated by their vibrant rhythm and uniqueness of presentation that we followed them as they engaged the crowds. I noticed waves of people were drawn out of their homes spontaneously. The atmosphere was filled with such a buzz of celebration, anticipation, and excitement! It was obvious the band's rhythm flowed out of their unified hearts through their instruments. This created an on-the-spot ecosystem for community and connection.

I began to ponder, wow, what they created is powerful and synergistic! I remember, after seeing them, asking myself questions like, what if businesses and organizations tapped into the power of rhythm? What if a leader could take all the moving parts and synergistically interconnect

1

them into a harmonious rhythm? The band distinguished themselves with a sound and interaction that was definitely intentional. Noticing the ecosystem they created was magnetic, drawing many people out of their homes spontaneously! It was something so very special that was taking place at that moment. It was like all our hearts connected to the rhythm of the sound that was released. Their creative brilliance was contagious!

This band broke the glass ceiling like pacesetters, fueling all of us to tap into something bigger than ourselves. Over the years of working with thousands of leaders nationally and internationally, I've noticed that we all have lenses, mindsets, reference points, or a worldview from which we see situations. Research shows we make most of our decisions from these reference points. This marching band's rhythm and sound created awareness that the neighbors longed for connection and community. Their gifted sound drew a spontaneous response that brought all walks of life together. It was so organic and truly remarkable to be a part of how this band effectively engaged the community.

As a coach, my heart with this book is to create awareness of the limitless power of tapping into rhythm. Think of the questions in this book being like a coach on the sidelines awakening and catapulting you to your full potential. Like the marching band having cues to adapt and pivot while engaging the crowds, you will also learn to adjust and seize the moment. Hearing the heart cry from many leaders trying to figure out how to constantly harmonize all the moving parts simultaneously, I can relate to their frustrations. After reading over a thousand books on business, growth, and leadership, I was able to connect the dots, to illustrate and unlock many treasures of influence from rhythm, and show you how to do this also.

My intention is to help you cultivate solutions, along with new habit patterns, and tap into the potential to incorporate all the moving parts like this band did to lead in the moment effectively. I noticed the marching band was having fun purposefully inspiring each other yet with on-point focus. This book is filled with ideas, inspiration, and innovative applications for you to carry your unique sound.

Seeing this high school band awaken a small town spontaneously, Synergistic Rhythm will provide a fresh perspective and inspire you to reimagine your approach to a thriving ecosystem. The marching band put their rhythm into action and on display. This book will foster action of key principles to empower you through the waves of uncertainty and chaos and leverage your full capacity. The band really didn't know what to expect, but their unified rhythm spoke for itself and was very attractive. Whatever your goals and vision are now, what's possible, infusing them with a synergistic strategy that's collaborative to scale your brand?

Just as a band has a team of directors and choreographers, it's an honor for me to take you through the seemingly complex and overwhelming components of leading and illustrate in a practical and applicable way how to apply synergistic rhythm. A successful band practices privately before they perform publicly. Think of this book as your time of preparation to tap into the vast potential of rhythm. A band has many people who are gifted with different instruments. I invite you to consider taking your team on a collaborative journey through this book, fostering the power of rhythm. The secret sauce of rhythm can be like rocket fuel launching and carrying the rocket to its desired destination.

From the band we saw, it was obvious their leadership team was able to interconnect various talents, practice, and then empower to action a harmonious rhythm that brought people together. One of the unique moments was when the different drummers turned and faced each other in the middle of the street, like a drum line, and were able to be in sync, focused, carrying a rhythm that literally captured your heart! It is a powerful thing to have a team of people leading in their area of expertise with such a united rhythm! Their confident synergy was like a grand finale during fireworks.

Whatever your leadership role is in business or your organization, no matter what you're facing, there is a solution! My encouragement to you as you are reading this book is to write in the margins, underline, and take active notes tapping into your solutions.

Like the band that captured my heart, may this book ignite you and inspire you to go further than you thought possible! My hope is that you and your team shine your unique rhythm in the world, being that catalyst for making a difference and bringing contribution.

Create your way to a better day. You got what it takes.

My Story of Hope

The Power of Forgiveness

A Defining Personal Moment

My heart is that if you're working through an addiction, abuse, abandonment, or a relationship that is estranged, my desire is that my personal journey will give you hope.

I grew up for 21 years in a home with an abusive, alcoholic father. My mom always did the best she could to raise my sister and me despite our circumstances. Then, when I turned 18 years old, she said, "Today, I am leaving your father and moving out of this home, and I waited until you were an adult so you could take care of yourself."

For seven years, we lived in the small city of Lancaster, Pennsylvania, and then moved to a small shack that became our home. It was outside the city, near a farm along a creek. I lived there until I was 21 years old. From 4th grade to my junior year in high school, I volunteered most days working on an Amish farm. No, I was not Amish, but they embraced me like one of their own. Their love, kindness, and acceptance marked my life forever! I am forever grateful for the skills and values I learned from working on the farm.

Sleeping in a Car

I can remember many nights my mom would run into our bedroom, saying in a panic, grab your pillows; we need to get out of the house! We would then hurry out at night in our pajamas to the car. Then, my mom would go park on a city street many times in front of her sister's home, and we would sleep in the parked car.

Sitting on the Step at Night

As a child, it was very difficult growing up living in an abusive, alcoholic home. My mom just had a way of coping every day and protecting us. I owe my mom my life. The verbal abuse and physical violence were many times so tumultuous after I would come home from working on the farm. I could hear the loud arguments along with fighting, and my body would tremble, and welts from fear would break out all over my body. I would continue sitting outside on the upper steps, listening to my dad fight with my mom. I would sit there night after night on the top step, shaking in fear. After my dad would fall asleep, I would go in the door and say, "Mom, how are you?"

She would always say, "I am good. Go to bed."

Our Perspective When We Smell Manure

Working on the farm, I would come home smelling like cow manure, and because of the home riddled with fear and abuse, many times, I would avoid a shower to not see my dad and sneak into my bed and quickly fall asleep. I would get up early, and my sister and I would leave for the school bus. I didn't realize, at times, that I would smell like cow manure and be made fun of, bullied, and called names for four straight years. My reaction out of self-protection was to stuff and avoid many types of conflict in an unhealthy way. I didn't realize I was building lots of internal anger, frustration, and feeling isolated. My view of conflict was from an abusive perspective. I tended to stuff challenges and become a doormat in many cases.

The fear and anxiety were intense, which led to my underage drinking and many other unwise choices. Growing up in this environment, I remember a boiling point when my dad arrived back at the job site many times drunk, very boisterous, and full of vernacular. I was running a crew on a three-story roof, and my dad immediately started criticizing me for the 1,000th time.

A Boiling Point

He got in my face. I got in his face. I thought in my heart, *This is it.* I had wild thoughts racing through my mind to "bear tackle" my dad and take us both off the roof and end this once and for all. But looking into my dad's amazing blue eyes, I felt a love and compassion that pierced my heart because he was my dad. I screamed and ran towards the ladder, hurried off the roof, and got in my vehicle crying, thinking, *What was I about to do?* Squealing my tires down the street, pounding my steering wheel, and sobbing… Little did I know I was being set up for a miracle.

Gold in the Sacrifice

My mom made a decision to send my sister and I to a private school. To help my mom with the tuition, I would stay after school daily, cleaning classrooms to pay our tuition. I remember getting sick many times and feeling awkward because I had to take special classes for a reading comprehension disability. Since my dad would spend all the money, I would do side jobs and whatever it took to help out my mom when I could put food on the table. I was a quiet, shut-down young boy who tried to avoid conflict whenever possible.

The Gift of Work

From working on the farm, I was fortunate to learn a great work ethic and be very gifted with my hands. I loved the farming experience and building things, so I pursued carpentry and did many side jobs. At age 18, I bought my first piece of land and, at age 22, built my first house for Patty and our future family, all while working a full-time construction job. I was very thankful for learning a skill at an early age.

The Power of Forgiveness

Fast forward to when I was 27, I had a spiritual encounter with God that transformed my heart towards my dad. About six months later, I made a choice to go to my father's home. As I was driving there, I remember experiencing such peace towards my father. For 27 years, I was trapped in unforgiveness, abandonment, and broken promises with my dad. I drove back a long, bumpy stone lane and parked at my dad's place. I was uncertain how to start our conversation but was experiencing such calmness and certainty. When I was walking down the very steps where I would shake in fear and break out in welts, I felt such a divine peace again.

Freedom from Forgiving

My dad was working in the yard, and I said, "Dad, I'd like to talk to you."

My dad stood up and walked toward me as we stood face-to-face on the sidewalk. I shared with him, "I know we have been through a lot over the past 20-plus years. The reason I am here is to take a moment and share my heart with you. I am here to share, from the depth of my heart, Dad, I forgive you!"

Accepting Forgiveness

My dad looked at me in silence, which seemed to be forever. He said, "Ed, how could you forgive me for all that I have done to you and our family?"

I said, "Dad, I'm here because my heart transformed toward you! Dad, I have fully forgiven you!"

He looked directly into my eyes the entire time. As my dad was processing and accepting my forgiveness, it was like time stood still for us. It was very peaceful.

I reiterated, "Dad, I fully forgive you, and not only forgive you, but I bless you as your son. I accept you as my father, and I release you from all that you have done to me and our family."

My dad paused for a moment. I could tell he was soaking in this divine moment of love, and then, simultaneously, we both reached out to hug each other!

The Power of a Hug

My dad and I hugged as we were both in our T-shirts on a hot summer day. Both of our shirts were saturated in each other's salty tears. The sense of peace, joy, and freedom filled our hearts as we cried. It was so healing for both of us. My dad and I went on an extraordinary journey as I accepted him as my father! I chose not to unscramble the cooked eggs and live from the past, but to look forward, start fresh, and build a new life with my dad! He had quit drinking and stayed completely dry and sober for over 25 years until the day he passed away.

Trauma to Triumph

My dad was someone I could always call and ask any questions about life or business. He taught me so much wisdom and insight about business and people. I asked my dad many questions over the years. He was my person to go to when I needed advice. We used to go to the local greasy spoon diner and enjoy countless breakfasts and black coffee together. Recently, while writing this book, I stopped by that diner and had breakfast by myself, reflecting on all the moments and memories of my father.

There is a Promise and a Hope

No matter what situation you're going through, I want to encourage you not to give up—don't quit. My dad and I ended up becoming best friends after 20-plus years of abuse. That's the power of forgiveness. I realized I was waiting for my dad to improve before I forgave him, and then I realized forgiveness sets me free. My dad and I became beneficiaries of the gift of forgiveness. My heart shifted towards my father, and I was very blessed to have almost three decades of getting to know and appreciate him. My dad would always say, "There is always a solution."

A Reflective Moment

Maybe you have a dad, mom, sibling, relative, or someone with whom you have been estranged for years. All I can say from my own journey is when I forgave my father, it set me free personally. At first, I was waiting for my dad to get his life together. Still, I realized it was my own unforgiveness that kept me in prison until it seemed hopeless, even impossible, but a miracle moment took place with an active decision to forgive.

This book, *Synergistic Rhythm*, is packed with many different true stories, and my heart is they would inspire you to not quit, to get back up one more time, to reach out for help, to encourage you not to go it alone, and to go further than you ever thought was possible.

CHAPTER ONE

Synergistic Rhythm

Synergistic Rhythm

What is possible with *Synergistic Rhythm*? Do you find yourself constantly hitting walls due to an offbeat rhythm? Are you unsure about the next steps to scale your business? Do you grapple with finding the right momentum, zone, lane, harmony, or sweet spot for your business, organization, or personal life? In this book, we delve into the potential of growing your business, organization, and life through Synergistic Rhythm.

Having spent multiple decades in business and nonprofits, and after traveling internationally to train numerous leaders and organizational heads, I've discovered that establishing Synergistic Rhythm within your systems, people, and culture can significantly drive dynamic growth. Learn to inspire your leaders, team, and clients, and elevate your brand and customer service to thrive in a world teeming with opportunities.

Unlocking Treasures with Questions

During this first chapter and future chapters, you may have questions. I believe questions are keys to unlocking many treasures of discovery. If you've ever hired a great coach, they have a way of being in the moment with you, creating a judgment-free space of growth and advancement, and asking many powerful questions. The questions positioned throughout this book are to foster growth and explore what may be possible. Think of them as moments of pause and reflection. I heard it said that we may be one question away from a pivotal moment in our destiny. What if the great inventors of our time stopped asking questions?

Searching for Rhythm Raising Our Family

I can remember my wife, Patty, rocking our firstborn son, Matthew, who enjoyed the rhythm of rocking. When he would cry, he seemed to almost magically respond immediately to the embrace of his mother and the rhythmic movement from rocking. There was always something so peaceful and comforting from her rocking all three of our children.

In our home, raising three children, we had lots going on with homeschooling, sports, music, and family activities. As we were raising our family, they all played music, and at first, the rhythm sounded interesting. For example, you could play at the other end of the house. At times, the frustration would cause someone to want to stop practicing, but their mom's nudge was empowering for them to keep going. As they grew in their talents playing their instruments, we all noticed their rhythm grow, and the sounds from their instruments captivated us and drew us in. They all play instruments and sing today.

At first, learning rhythm may be frustrating, like it was for our children learning their songs, but I want to encourage you that as you grow in your leadership rhythm, many will be drawn to you and what you do. Finding your business and organizational rhythm is possible, and when you find this rhythm, it will be like a plane carrying everyone simultaneously toward the purpose. As you're exploring how rhythm works and how to apply rhythm, I want to encourage you to consider this book like a flight crew flying you to your destination.

Awareness and Intentionality

Awareness and intentionality are crucial to fostering and nurturing a thriving Synergistic Rhythm. We will discuss how to implement and magnify your growth potential using Synergistic Rhythm. Through this book, you'll be equipped to take decisive action, reclaim control, and bolster your growth momentum.

Having been in business for several decades and trained countless business leaders globally, I empathize with those sleepless nights, the pressures of meeting payroll, and the overarching feeling of being overwhelmed. Business is not for the faint-hearted. However, understanding how to create and maintain Synergistic Rhythm can be transformative for you, both personally and professionally.

Solving Growth Pain Points

This book aims to equip business owners and organizational leaders with insights to apply potent strategies to address major pain points in leading and growing a thriving enterprise. It offers inspiration and practical advice for leaders, managers, entrepreneurs, and executives to intentionally drive growth.

Benefits of Synergistic Rhythm

Implementing Synergistic Rhythm offers fundamental benefits, including maximizing the effectiveness and efficiency of your business and organization, augmenting value in client or customer experiences, and boosting sales, customer, and employee retention. It fosters a collaborative culture, optimizing skills, roles, resources, innovation, time, and energy. What value would you attribute to reduced conflicts, minimized stress, and fewer repeated mistakes?

Imagine having your entire team, with all its resources, time, and energy, aligned toward fulfilling the vision, mission, and purpose. Synergistic Rhythm is vibrant, invigorating, and harmonious, touching all facets of your business. Can you envision the artistic and scientific sides of leadership converging to achieve consistently outstanding results? This book will inspire you to innovate and expand, guiding you through this potent process to establish a dynamically effective enterprise.

"Transitioning a business from current state to future state requires clear strategy, adaptability, synergy among all involved and a dedication to execution - among other things."
~ Hendrith Vanlon Smith Jr

Have you ever wondered what constitutes a thriving business? How do they integrate what appears intangible with the tangible? We often hear terms like branding, teams, systems, culture, and core values. In this context, we will delve into these concepts and understand how they mesh together in a Synergistic Rhythm. This goes beyond a mere formula; it's an intentional rhythm that drives and energizes your business's purpose, vision, and mission.

In this book, we will look at solutions for:

1. Dealing with isolation.
2. Overcoming indecision
3. Knowing the next steps to take
4. Managing cash flow

5. Dealing with Conflict
6. Managing life's priorities
7. Dealing with distractions
8. Hiring and retention
9. Managing the mind
10. Scaling your business growth
11. Knowing your no
12. Growing your systems, people, and culture

Let's define both Synergistic and Rhythm.

Synergistic:

According to the Cambridge Dictionary, synergy is described as "causing or involving synergy (the combined power of working together that is greater than the power achieved by working separately): the synergistic effect of two drugs given at the same time."

In this book, we will take vital key components, apply them synergistically, and create a harmonious rhythm to intentionally grow and lead with effectiveness.

"Rhythm is one of the principal translators between dream and reality."
~ Edith Sitwell

Rhythm:

Cambridge:
1. A regular movement or pattern of movements.
2. Regular pattern of change, especially one that happens in **nature**.

Vocabulary.com

1. Use the noun rhythm to refer to the regular pattern of something in a cycle or the beat in a song. In the summer, your life takes on a different rhythm than during the school year.

2. Rhythm comes from the Greek rhythmos "measured movement, flow." The beat of a song or the meter of a poem is its rhythm.

3. You can also describe the cycle of things that happen in life or nature, like the ocean tide or the passing of the seasons, as a rhythm.

4. If you have no rhythm, you're not very good at dancing.

5. And once your favorite basketball team has found its rhythm, you know it's going to win.

Synergistic Rhythm:

Ed Garner's Definition:

"Multiple components working together at a defined pace consistently producing desired results. An ongoing pattern of success with many variables in motion simultaneously."

Rhythm in Nature

Nature serves as a magnificent example of rhythm. In all its splendor, nature presents an ecosystem where numerous elements work harmoniously together, supporting life on multiple levels. Have you ever stepped outside, taken a moment to pause, and felt an overwhelming sense of calm and tranquility? It seems that everything in nature operates with a seasonal rhythm. The four seasons interconnect and intertwine in intricate ways to support a continuously thriving ecosystem that sustains life on Earth. What lessons can we glean from nature to apply to our businesses?

We thrive when immersed in nature's ecosystem. Imagine if your business could seamlessly integrate systems, culture, and people in such a flourishing manner that most remain oblivious to the intricate workings, just as nature does for us.

Have you ever wondered why we are drawn outdoors, relishing the warmth of the sun, breathing in the fresh air, and admiring nature's vibrant hues? Numerous wellness benefits stem from nature's **rhythmic ecosystem**. But what if your business could emulate a similar **rhythmic ecosystem** where people, systems, culture, and core values collaborate intentionally? Imagine a place where emergencies, unnecessary drama, time-wasters, and inefficiencies were curtailed. What rhythm-related solution could address your most pressing pain point? Which systems could adapt, adjust, and enhance processes to foster a consistent **rhythmic ecosystem**? What remains your team's most formidable challenge or pain point?

To put it another way, have you observed how nature anticipates the coming season? It prepares for the next phase with deliberate harmony. What if a systematic rhythm could aid you in priming and propelling your business into its next phase? Consider asking daily: What's functioning well? What isn't? This book aims to help you assess your major pain points, viewing them as stepping stones to broader growth. Think about obtaining feedback from your team and customers and transforming those pain points into opportunities for expansion. How can systems encapsulate the essence of your business culture? Remember, whatever is tolerated eventually becomes the culture!

Exploratory Questions

1. Ask yourself why most emergencies in business happen.

2. Why do so many things just pop up, causing delays and profit loss?

3. Is it because there hasn't been a thoughtful, systematic rhythm with the systems, team, and culture?

4. Is there a squeaky wheel that keeps making noise that must be addressed?

5. Many times, we hear frustrations with leaders saying, if it would not be for the people, I would enjoy business.

6. What if people are actually the greatest asset within a thriving business? What is actually possible after establishing an interconnected culture that each teammate carries the company vision and culture because they want to?

Rhythm in Franchises

Have you ever wondered why certain franchises seem more effective than others? Could it be due to a Synergistic Rhythm? What stands out to you about the most successful franchisees? What systematic approaches regarding people, systems, culture, and core values can you discern? How about their personal development training, the efficiency of their systems, or the alignment of personality and cultural values, all operating in tandem to achieve the mission, purpose, and vision?

Synchronization in Ice Skating

Have you ever been captivated by a figure skater gracefully moving and dancing in rhythm with the music? Or by a pair of skaters so harmoniously synchronized that their performance resembles a poetic masterpiece? The spectacle's brilliance stems from countless hours of behind-the-scenes practice, coaching, and dedication. Their impeccable timing and synchronization with the music make the performance seem effortlessly perfect. What lessons can we draw for businesses?

Commitment to Excellence

Skaters commit to excellence, establishing daily habits that consistently drive them towards excellence. Their regimen encompasses not just skating but also mindset training, wellness, physical exercise, ballet, and heeding expert coaching. They cultivate an environment and ecosystem to support them both on and off the ice. Their hard work culminates in live performances executed with near-perfect harmony.

Consider this: many will pay to watch others achieve something extraordinary. What is so exceptional about your business that clients will seek your services? What underlying business purpose keeps you going, even when facing challenges? Why do customers choose your products or services over similar companies? What differentiates you, enabling you to offer gold medal-worthy service? When you "step onto the ice" with live music, what drives you, your team, and your company to deliver performances that earn standing ovations?

Metronome

What exactly is a metronome? According to Wikipedia, "A metronome is a device that produces an audible click or other sound at a regular interval set by the user, typically in beats per minute. Metronomes may include synchronized visual motion. Musicians use the device to practice playing to a regular pulse." What would a regular pulse resemble in your systems, culture, relationships, and core values? Which systems currently implement the metronomic principle in your business? Are you receiving any feedback from your customers or team to fine-tune the rhythm? What measures can you adopt to establish the right rhythm with systems, culture, people, and core values? If you're wondering where to begin, this book offers numerous practical applications and real-life inspirational stories.

Set the Metronome

We can intentionally set the metronome, so to speak, through our **Systems, Culture, People, and Core Values.** Not having a plan then actually becomes a plan. Like with music, there are different beats. As a leader, we can set the tone and culture to carry the synchronized rhythm. Constantly getting feedback from your team and customers on what's working and not working is so important. Your customers are a part of your team.

S.C.P.V

For the purposes of this book, let's refer to Systems, Culture, People, and Core Values as S.C.P.V. We will dive deeper into each area in this book. These are four pillars to build your business and organization on with Synergistic Rhythm.

Monitor Your Metronome

What is your personal, business, and organizational metronome? How can you synergistically set the rhythm with intentionality and consistency? A metronome has to be turned on and set so everyone listening plays their instrument and sings with a synergistic beat. In what ways can you interconnect your **S.C.P.V.** to a metronome? Like vehicles have dashboard lights, how could you set up dashboard lights to give you feedback, helping to support everyone with the right click of the metronome? Consider doing an idea exchange with your team to process your dashboard to measure and monitor your metronome.

Understanding Timing and Pace

One of the lessons we can learn to have Synergistic Rhythm is there is the right timing and pace—the timing and pace that comes with integrating the different components of your business. It's possible to have many people playing different instruments but all in tune with the rhythm of the metronome. What could be your business metronome? How could you uniquely connect your teams and customers to your business metronome? What is your healthy timing and pace to carry the core values and vision with the right culture?

Hot Air Balloon Timing and Pace

I remember eagerly waiting for the day the hot air balloon pilot would tell us to be at the park at 5 a.m. He was timing it based on the weather, winds, and temperature. I never realized how large the balloon was until it was fully in the air. I thought, *Wow, and I'm going to trust a complete stranger and an apparatus I've never seen before?* Then, the pilot announced that we were ready to get in the basket. As the heat from the tanks filled the balloon, we lifted off, and before I knew it, we were 3,000 feet in the air. The pace of the balloon was determined by adjusting the altitude to capture different wind currents. The pilot would either raise or lower the balloon to catch these currents. Since we were moving with the wind, we felt no resistance—it was a perfect rhythm. The pilot constantly communicated with the chase vehicle in case of an emergency. His choice of timing was based on the weather and conditions, while the balloon's pace was determined by its altitude. Flying over our local city and seeing things from such a unique perspective was truly extraordinary.

Balloon Lessons Learned

1. The pilot prepared all the equipment in advance.
2. The timing was chosen based on weather, instruments, and calculations.
3. The pilot and crew were there early to prepare for the customers.
4. The pilot was light-hearted and carried confidence, which we then felt more safe and secure.
5. He was able to slow the speed of the balloon down based on altitude.
6. Constant communication with a chase vehicle with potential landing sites.
7. I noticed when we were flying over houses, we could hear their sound amplified, hearing every word.
8. The whole experience was very calming and relaxing, and it felt rhythmic.

Power of the Huddle

We've all seen our favorite football teams huddle between plays. A lot can be accomplished during a huddle: new plays introduced, high-fives exchanged, mindset shifts, and adjustments made in response to the opposing team. Most athletic teams place great value on these huddles. In fact, games can be won or lost based on what happens in the huddle.

Now, imagine consistently having daily, weekly, and monthly huddles. Consider the value you could bring into each meeting as you benchmark growth, celebrate wins, and establish rhythm. How could these huddles make your team more efficient and effective? Without them, connections can erode, potentially compromising the longevity and health of your team.

Consider empowering your team by incorporating a few powerful questions into your huddles. Think about a business where employees and associates are valued beyond just the financial aspect. The huddle can foster greater value, loyalty, and retention in their hearts and minds.

Questions to Consider for a Huddle

1. What is working on the team?
2. How are the overall systems going?
3. What are the customers saying?
4. How can we as a team grow our unity and harmony?
5. What is working well?
6. How can we pivot and adapt to current market conditions?

Company Culture Tempo

In music, "tempo" refers to the speed at which a musical instrument is played. Artists and musicians adjust the metronome to achieve the precise speed or feel they desire for their music. For example, sad songs tend to be played slowly, while fast-paced songs are often more upbeat. Tempo and rhythm can also be combined to create livelier music.

Tempo can be likened to the feel or vibe of a company. Let's equate tempo with business culture. The tempo provides customers or clients with a specific experience of your company and the customer experience. In other words, is it a fast-paced environment or a slower one? When people engage with your brand, they experience a certain "tempo," so to speak. This encompasses the entire journey, from the initial introduction to the point where the customer fully receives your product or service.

Team Tempo

Consider your team; each individual might have their own tempo and rhythm. When combined, these unique rhythms can create a sort of symphony. What if you could shift, develop, or place people into different roles to enhance this Synergistic Rhythm? Imagine combining a pianist with a guitarist, then adding a drummer and a saxophonist. The tempo and overall experience transform with the addition of various instruments.

It's essential to be clear on the vision, mission, purpose, and core values. This clarity allows you to set the right tempo for every customer and employee experience. With consistency, you'll empower your people, enrich the customer experience, and boost retention, creativity, security, innovation, and profits.

Consider a track star at the starting line. When they hear the signal, they sprint off, setting a tempo that allows them to finish strong. Their heart rate increases to supply their muscles with oxygen-rich blood. However, they can't maintain this rapid heart rate indefinitely without risking exhaustion. Everyone has a sustainability threshold determined by various factors. What's the optimal pace for your team?

Capacity

Understanding the capacity of individuals and the team as a whole is crucial for setting the right Synergistic Rhythm. The great news is that once you recognize potential synergies and combine them effectively, your perspective shifts. For instance, after buying a blue vehicle of a particular model, I began seeing that model everywhere. My awareness expanded, and it felt like a veil had been lifted. Enhancing capacity could start by showing your team alternative, more efficient ways of doing things.

As bands practice, they establish a tempo that brings their music to life. Similarly, in business, cultivating a culture of learning, growth, and inspired leadership can amplify your operational tempo. With increased capacity, both effectiveness and efficiency become more achievable. Embrace new ideas and empower creativity.

Capacity

Expanding capacity is akin to removing a lid from a container and filling it. Consider identifying limiting factors or constraints in your operations. For instance, a tire with a slow puncture might need refilling every few days. Addressing and repairing this issue can lead to extended tire life. Recognizing these "leaks" or constraints is essential to innovate and devise solutions. Reflect on the limiting factors within your business, including your systems, people, culture, and core values. Recognizing them is crucial because, once addressed, they could pave the way for growth.

Establish Roles

One method to fine-tune rhythm and identify capacity issues is to clearly define roles for each team member. Reflect on how each role interconnects to ensure no one operates in isolation. How do these roles enable individuals to excel? Understanding their strengths, gifts, personalities, and talents can profoundly benefit both them and the business. To boost efficiency and develop a harmonious business rhythm, place individuals in roles that they're passionate about and align with their strengths.

Questions to consider:

1. Does your team understand their role?
2. Does your team know their role?
3. When they're in that role, does that person come alive?

4. How could you invest in their growth?
5. How could you add value to their roles?

Conformity

Your capacity to expand can often be hindered by the pressure to conform or stick to what is familiar. The challenge of conformity begins with personal mindsets and extends to team and organizational leaders and managers. Venturing into uncharted territory might demand a fresh approach, adjustments, and a pivot in thinking.

What exactly does conformity mean? It's an agreement with a standard. How can this impede capacity? By aligning with a standard that doesn't promote growth or profit. For instance, an entitlement mindset and an incentive mindset are polar opposites, yet both can adhere to a standard. What if it's feasible to cultivate a Synergistic Rhythm that promotes growth, encourages initiative, and rewards behaviors moving in the right direction?

Negative conformity can manifest as: "This is how we've always done it, so why change?" Such thinking within an organization creates an adverse rhythm, stifling the growth of ideas, innovation, and collaborative endeavors. To use an analogy, consider a pond accumulating algae versus a flowing river. Both conform to their banks, but while the river continually moves and nourishes its surroundings, the stagnant pond allows algae to thrive.

Define Constraints

Identifying your business constraints and understanding their root causes can be immensely beneficial for business growth. Contemplating solutions to these constraints can add substantial value, ultimately enhancing customer service. What impedes growth or consistently frustrates your team, system, or culture?

Let's illustrate a constraint. On the East Coast of the United States, there's an interstate highway called I-95. If you've traveled on it, you've likely encountered extensive traffic jams. Once, while heading south, the four lanes gradually reduced to one, causing a massive bottleneck. The reason? Workers were scraping paint off steel for repainting. At a glance, one might blame the workers for the jam, but is that the root cause?

Root or Symptom?

Upon reflection and after consulting a steel painting expert, I considered that the real cause might have been inadequate paint preparation. Could the traffic jams have been prevented with proper prep techniques before painting? While it's uncertain, this contemplation shifted my perspective toward understanding the genuine root causes of business constraints and disruptions in rhythm. Often, visible issues in your business might be mere symptoms, not the actual root constraints.

Misunderstanding Leads to Constraints

Looking internally at a business, suppose there's a recurring human resource issue. Could the root of this problem lie in the initial hiring process, role definition, core values, or approach to the systems, culture, and people within the organization? Do new hires fully grasp the company's mission, values, vision, and operational approach? Could many challenges be alleviated by enhancing training, setting clearer expectations, and offering comprehensive evaluations in an employee's first 90 days?

Questions to Consider:

1. What constraints continually show up in your business?
2. What is the actual root cause of the constraint?
3. Is there an area of your business where there is an assumption in operation?
4. In other words, does everyone understand what you're saying and communicating, and how it applies?

CHAPTER TWO

Rhythm Rooted in Core Values

Business Core Values

Let's delve into the intricacies of achieving Synergistic Rhythm. Have you ever pondered the unique ingredient that makes a business stand out? At the foundation of business choices, activities, employee retention, and profit prioritization lie core values. Implementing the right core values can spur growth, delineating clear boundaries and priorities. Envision core values as our biological heart—they nourish every facet of the business and also shield it.

We'll discuss how core values can work synergistically, creating a rhythm reminiscent of a meticulously maintained engine. For a rudimentary analogy, consider the pistons in an engine. These pistons, crucial components hidden from plain sight, represent the integral parts of a mechanism. If your vehicle is low on oil, you might hear a piston knock in an older engine, a sound that, if ignored, could lead to engine failure.

Culture Carrying Core Values

Picture the pistons being surrounded by oil. In this analogy, the oil symbolizes your company's culture. A robust culture, when infused with intent by every team member, carries the core values, fueling the synergistic rhythm. Just as oil is vital, culture profoundly impacts all business dimensions.

For an engine to function efficiently, all its pistons must operate in harmony, propelling the vehicle towards its destination. Now, think about the exciting potential of embarking on a transformative journey to understand your engine oil—your culture—and how it can uphold your core values, which are the lifeblood of your enterprise.

The Heart - Core Values

What principle lies at the center of your business? In other words, what do people frequently remark about the owner, leaders, or the business itself? What positive, energizing feedback do they offer about your team? Allocate some time over the next 30 days to reflect on the essence of your business—your core values. Engage in an enlightening exchange where you brainstorm five or more foundational, one-word core values.

Then, invest time to define these values in your vernacular, in terms your team resonates with, and take note of the insights. Ponder on how to actualize each value innovatively. Core values should inspire a grander mission for your squad. Once deeply ingrained at the heart and mindset level, individuals will exude these values, even subconsciously.

Priorities and Boundaries

Let's contemplate the essence of time in understanding our priorities and boundaries. Core values aid in crystallizing these aspects. The business world will incessantly demand your time. Often, I'm questioned about time management. Reframe this to think of "priority management" rather than just managing time. Which growth-centric activity could set the pace for your business rhythm? If you devoted time to this particular activity, could it catalyze your business's expansion?

"The key is not to prioritize what's on your schedule, but to schedule your priorities."~ Stephen Covey

Growth Activities vs. Management Activities

We've all heard the adage, "working on your business versus working in your business." Think of growth activity as making a sales call and management activity as balancing your checkbook. Both are essential, but without growth activities like sales, there won't be a checkbook to balance. Core values can enhance excellence in these areas as well. Often, business owners can become bogged down in management, causing growth activities to suffer. For instance, to maintain a thriving rhythm and maximize our time, we need two primary elements: time priority and time boundary.

Growth Priorities

Prioritizing ensures we remain result-driven, while boundaries protect our business, values, and goals and shield us from distractions and time wasters. Consider listing the top five growth activities that, when consistently executed, make your business thrive. Ask yourself: what hinders these growth activities?

Recalling my time working on a farm, we prepared the soil, fixed equipment, and mended the barn. But imagine if we never got around to sowing seeds. We might boast of a pristine barn, impeccable machinery, and fertile land. Yet, in ninety days, we'd be faced with a weed-infested field rather than a cultivated crop. While weeds merely cover the ground, crops provide seeds and income for the year. What single action could you initiate to sow seeds into the soil of your business's systems, people, and culture?

"You have to decide what your highest priorities are and have the courage—pleasantly, smilingly, unapologetically, to say 'no' to other things. And the way you do that is by having a bigger 'yes' burning inside. The enemy of the 'best' is often the "good." ~ *Stephen Covey*

Know Your No

In the context of setting priorities and boundaries, consider the practicality of implementation. Business core values help determine your "YES" and your "NO." Picture an artist painting on a canvas: anything outside the canvas represents your "no," while painting within its boundaries signifies your "yes." Establishing the right core values on this canvas clarifies what to respond to affirmatively. Your business's Systems, People, and Culture are all unified by Core Values. Are your team members familiar with these core values? Do they understand the daily priorities essential for business growth and expansion? Are they aligned with the mission?

"Your ability to select your most important task at each moment, and then to get started on that task and to get it done both quickly and well, will probably have more of an impact on your success than any other quality or skill you can develop." ~ *Brian Tracy*

Core Value Rhythm

The rhythm created by your core values will drive your overall business rhythm. Synergistic Rhythm harmonizes your business and personal culture. Often, stress and subpar results arise from incongruities with core values. Every business organization aiming for Synergistic Rhythm should be clear about its core values. Truly understanding these values goes beyond mere cognitive awareness. It's more about a deep, heartfelt, or intuitive grasp. Take, for example, the core value of "world-class customer service." While "service" can be a core value in itself, there's a distinction between basic service and top-tier, five-star service.

Defining Your Core Values

To bolster growth in your business and foster a strong organizational culture, it's crucial to clearly define your core values. These values will influence every facet of your business. Without this clarity and definition, your core values, culture, and rhythm risk becoming ambiguous or left to assumption. Core values articulate the essence of your business's existence—they underscore the primary reasons your business operates.

"Don't be a time manager, be a priority manager. Cut your major goals into bite-sized pieces. Each small priority or requirement on the way to the ultimate goal becomes a mini goal in itself." ~ Denis Waitley

Practical Action Steps to Consider

1. The first step is to have fun and list on a tablet as many one-word positive attributes you want to see in your business.
2. Do your best to list out twelve or more core values.
3. Avoid copying other companies' core values; what works is your authenticity.
4. Then, set a timer for 30 seconds and circle the first eight attributes that jump off the page to you.
5. Now, in your own words, define them in one sentence.
6. If you have a core team of leaders, invite them to do this same exercise simultaneously; this way, there is no comparison.

7. Then ask them all to turn them in to you. This will give you valuable feedback.

8. After you have digested the feedback, highlight the common overlaps. They all knowingly or unknowingly experience the current culture and business core values.

9. To transform the culture and core values, we must first identify and define them.

10. Now, the refining takes time, along with your feedback, to define and redefine your core values and definitions.

11. Then, take time to print them out, gather your core team, and do a collaborative refining of actual core values and definitions.

12. After that, let it sit for one week, and revisit it with your team for the final draft.

The Implementation of Core Values

Display them prominently: post and print them in the office and online. Initiate discussions around them and listen to customer feedback. Then, importantly, recognize and celebrate team members who embody and communicate these values. I recall assisting a business with this enriching process; the sense of community and connection it fostered instilled a deeper purpose within the team's hearts. They grasped the larger significance of their existence within the organization.

Awareness

Acknowledge behaviors that align with these values. Regularly celebrate and honor team members — whether daily or weekly — who demonstrate these core values. This acknowledgment cultivates a connection between understanding the core value and its practical application. Observe how these values manifest within teams, throughout the company, and in customer service and sales.

Power of Intention

If you aim to distinguish your company or organization, intentionally implement your business's core values. These values represent the driving force behind the vision and purpose. They are the heartbeat and fuel of your business rhythm. When intention reaches a fervent level, it can reshape focus, influence choices, guide actions, and ultimately determine outcomes.

> *"The mark of a great man is one who knows when to set aside the important things in order to accomplish the vital ones."*
> *~ Brandon Sanderson*

What We Tolerate Becomes Culture

Think of culture as the leaven that raises dough when baking bread. While you can't necessarily see it in the dough once it's mixed in, you can observe its impact as the dough rises. Culture functions similarly; it amplifies the best of your vision and purpose. Whether teammates, coworkers, or customers, anyone interacting with your culture will experience it, for better or worse.

Synergy of Pistons Working Together

Many people seek balance, which may not truly exist. When people mention seeking balance, they are often actually searching for rhythm. Rhythm denotes healthy movement. For instance, stagnant ponds can develop algae, while flowing streams maintain healthier water. Thus, balance, in a beneficial sense, equates to rhythmic movement. Imagine if all core values moved synergistically in rhythm.

What if you could operate a business from a place of rest? Consider the image of a swan gracefully gliding across the water. People crave rest, but it's not about idleness; it's about movement from a state of peaceful existence. Have you ever observed someone walking heavily, as though their feet were stomping? Conversely, moving from a restful perspective means walking lightly, exuding a more commanding presence. Have you encountered someone whose mere presence illuminates a room? Their authentic alignment with their core values is evident, even without words.

Envision all your core values, operating simultaneously without contradiction. What if all your business core values harmoniously collaborated, driving your business vision and purpose to fruition?

"Synergy is everywhere in nature. If you plant two plants close together, the roots commingle and improve the quality of the soil so that both plants will grow better than if they were separated. If you put two pieces of wood together, they will hold much more than the total weight held by each separately. The whole is greater than the sum of its parts. One plus one equals three or more." ~ Stephen Covey

CHAPTER THREE

The Power of The Domino Effect

The Power of the Domino Effect

The domino effect begins with a single push of the first domino. This initial action triggers the second domino, and the sequence continues rhythmically until the last domino falls. Interestingly, for the domino effect to work effectively, there must be precise spacing between each piece. If the gap between any two dominos is too wide, the chain reaction halts. I remember being utterly captivated by dominos set up in intricate patterns, watching intently until the very end. A critical component of the domino effect is that initial action — setting the first domino in motion.

"The rhythm of daily action aligned with your goals creates the momentum that separates dreamers from super-achievers."
~ Darren Hardy

Proactive Action

Let's apply the domino effect to our **systems, people, culture,** and **core values** (S.P.C.V.). What could be the initiating domino in your business that, when nudged, sets off momentum, touching the second, third, and so forth? Consider introducing a core value as the first domino:

"celebration." Ponder the potential outcomes of celebrating a team member's achievements, be it a task completed with excellence or any action that aligns well with the vision. What if you celebrated a team member who just closed a sale? What could be the ripple effects of such a gesture? Think about starting with a domino that requires no monetary investment; when activated or acknowledged, it can have a profound ripple effect, positively influencing many facets of your business.

"Being proactive is more than taking initiative. It is recognizing that we are responsible for our own choices and have the freedom to choose based on principles and values rather than on moods or conditions. Proactive people are agents of change and choose not to be victims, to be reactive, or to blame others." ~ Stephen Covey

Shift from Analyzing to Action

One factor that can impede the domino effect is over-analyzing each domino. Put simply, who doesn't appreciate being celebrated? Recall a time when a colleague celebrated you—how did that make you feel? It's akin to the ripple created by a stone thrown into water. A key component of a thriving business rhythm is transformed individuals. Take a moment to consider your top five core values, and think about arranging them as your first five dominos. As one domino connects with the next, **it intertwines with your systems, people, and culture**. This domino effect then permeates those three main business pillars. Just as the sound of falling dominos captivates our attention, envision the potential of dynamic core values in action, enriching the culture within your business. What transformative influence could consistently setting up dominos within your business have, igniting a thriving rhythm?

"You'll never plough a field by turning it over in your mind."
~ Irish Proverb

Questions to Consider

1. What one step of action could you take to touch that domino?
2. How could you prepare your team for a consistent domino effect?
3. Where are the spaces too far apart and not able to reach the next domino?
4. Scaling your brand, how could you position your current resources to foster a domino effect?

Application With Consistency

One of the simplest yet most productive keys to success is consistency. When a leader is consistent, that alone can trigger a domino effect. For instance, consider the decision to walk a certain number of steps daily or the habit of consistently smiling or expressing gratitude. Such actions not only have a cumulative impact over three months but can also ripple out, influencing other areas of one's life. What could you do consistently every day that establishes the rhythm of a domino effect within your culture, impacting your customers? When you observe actual dominos connecting with each other, they produce a rhythmic sound. Sounds draw people in. One approach to maintaining consistency is to encourage your team to focus on one domino a week, such as fostering a culture of service. You might even venture to have them collectively decide on the domino for the following week. Over time, these dominos are aligned, driving the business rhythm synergistically.

"Motivation gets you going, but discipline keeps you growing. That's the Law of Consistency. It doesn't matter how talented you are. It doesn't matter how many opportunities you receive. If you want to grow, consistency is key." ~ John C. Maxwell

Consider Intentional Leadership

1. What process or protocol could you put in place for your team to keep rhythm consistent throughout your entire business?
2. What should you do when someone decides not to carry the culture?
3. Your people are your culture carriers; how could you empower them to be intentional in serving your clients and customers?
4. What training could be put in place to infuse the right culture into your culture carriers?
5. Which new processes would support the domino effect in your business?

Domino Effect With Habits

Habits are incredibly powerful! Think of them like the pillars of a bridge, supporting its structure. What's one new habit you could adopt to foster a Synergistic Rhythm? Consider starting with adjusting your attitude in response to situations and circumstances. If your attitude breeds frustration or negativity, it can impact the entire business culture.

Consider the historic bridge that spans the mile-wide Susquehanna River. Sometimes, I stand there, awed by the massive arched concrete pillars that consistently support the bridge, allowing people to reach their destinations. This serves as a metaphor for habits built to sustain your goals, vision, and purpose.

Now, think about your team. Imagine if you implemented one new habit each month for a year. What would the cumulative effect be five years down the line? For instance, consider the way the phone is answered or the manner in which customers are greeted upon arrival. The domino effect of establishing the right habits month by month can propel your business toward significant growth.

"Sometimes, all it takes is your smile (even if forced), and a domino effect of smiles happen... infectious." ~ Ace Antonio Hall.

The Domino Effect of Culture

I recently traveled from the East Coast to the West Coast with a business colleague and noticed a stark difference within the same airline: from one terminal to another, there was a complete shift in culture, approaches, and attitudes. This experience highlighted the power of the domino effect and the contrast between a healthy and a toxic culture.

A Few Dominoes Create Ripples

Traveling can be demanding—early mornings, adapting to new technology, and navigating updated protocols. At our first stop, we mistakenly stood in the security line, thinking it was the check-in line, until a fellow traveler pointed out our error. Then, in the actual airline baggage check-in line, we waited a long time, all the while hearing airline employees sharply reprimanding their customers. This aggressive approach set off a negative domino effect, escalating the frustration and agitation of those in line.

This culture wasn't customer-friendly or solution-oriented. The management's tolerance of these employees' negative behavior was both unproductive and costly. The experience was marred by a pervasive negativity. It seemed a few employees had an undue influence on the hundreds of people just trying to get to their gates.

Leadership Influences the Domino Effect

The return journey from the West Coast was a different story. The airport was filled with helpful staff positioned almost like concierges. They were calm, relaxed, and accommodating. Even though the lines were longer, they moved much faster than on the East Coast. It was evident that leadership had placed a priority on employee attitude and training.

Intentionally Setting Up Dominoes

These contrasting experiences underscored the vital role culture plays in executing a vision. The first experience was so off-putting it made me reconsider flying with that airline again, while the second left me eager to book another flight. Leadership's influence, for better or worse, was apparent. This journey highlighted the fact that different parts of the same company can offer vastly different experiences, impacting the overall growth of the company. Leaders must be intentional in evaluating, holding employees accountable, and providing training to nurture a positive culture.

The Placing of Dominoes

One significant takeaway was seeing how just a few individuals could negatively influence so many travelers at the East Coast airport. Conversely, on the West Coast, the strategic positioning of their team at bottleneck areas ensured efficient flow and a pleasant experience for travelers. This positive experience highlighted the importance of strategic leadership, which avoids making assumptions and ensures customers are clear about the next steps. The kind and service-minded attitudes of the staff made all the difference.

1. How could you intentionally place processes and systems to carry your business culture and potential bottlenecks?
2. How do we remove the big assumption from your business process?
3. What could you do to make your experience fun and exciting for your clients and customers?

Consider Intentional Leadership

1. What process or protocol could you put in place for your team to keep culture rhythm consistent throughout your entire business?
2. What should you do when someone decides not to carry the culture?
3. Your people are your culture carriers; how could you empower them to be intentional in serving your clients and customers?
4. What training could be put in place to infuse the right culture into your culture carriers?
5. What new processes would help carry your business domino effect?

Employee or Customer: Who Comes First?

Both are undeniably crucial. Reflecting on our experiences at the East Coast and West Coast airports, the number of customers wasn't the issue. Instead, our experiences were shaped by the airline's employees. Could it be that nurturing a thriving company culture, which prioritizes customer experience, actually leads to an increased customer base? Consider the potential growth if you invest in the right training, enabling your team to champion and perpetuate a healthy culture. The West Coast terminal clearly valued its customers, as evidenced by the highly trained, service-oriented employees. Thriving employees not only carry the company's culture but also act as ambassadors or salespeople for the brand. Their impact on business growth can be either positive or negative. And while intentional training is paramount, consistency remains the game changer.

Synergy of Dominos

Despite introducing brand-new technology we hadn't encountered before, the West Coast airline terminal ensured that operations ran smoothly. Their blending of new technology, systems, and culture allowed for the efficient movement of thousands of passengers, ushering them to their respective gates in a seamless rhythm. Think of a meticulously arranged domino setup: each piece is unique, but they all work synergistically, influencing each other right up to the last domino. The airline industry has seen numerous shifts. Our experience that day demonstrated how an airline can adapt and pivot, integrating new technology, people, and systems into a culture that ensures a pleasant experience for travelers.

Questions to Consider

1. What if the root of great customer service is actually a healthy, thriving team?
2. How could you become more effective in growing a healthy team culture?
3. What could you do consistently to add value to your employees, empowering them to go the extra mile?

Great Potential with the Domino Effect

The power of the domino effect holds great potential for increasing your sales, profits, and market share awareness. Consider tracking your dominos for fifty straight weeks and evaluating their effectiveness. Think about using and implementing dominos that cost very little but have a high impact.

Gathering feedback from your team and customers during this period can significantly fuel the domino effect. Remember, once all the dominos are positioned and the first domino is set into motion, it will trigger all the dominos in its path. Your potential for massive growth might just be one domino away.

Actions to Consider:

1. What one new habit could you implement this month?
2. During a huddle, ask the team what new habit they feel would fuel growth.
3. What habits would fuel a domino effect of business growth?

Transform the Domino Effect's Meaning

Perhaps you've heard of or experienced the domino effect in a negative context. For instance, observing a chain of events where one situation leads to another, potentially culminating in a catastrophic loss. Maybe you've adopted the belief that negative outcomes always happen, or you wonder when your break will come because bad things seem to keep happening. We've all heard about pessimists versus optimists or the debate about seeing a glass as half-empty versus half-full. But what if we could change our perspective on the meaning attached to an event or situation, turning it into a cascading positive domino effect? Even when setting up actual dominoes for a turn, they are arranged in a manner that resembles more of a sweep than a blunt 90° turn. What if every event, situation, or circumstance was simply feedback for a sweeping turnaround, altering the meaning, influence, and impact of the domino effect?

The Influence from the Turnaround

Take, for instance, my experience with the East Coast airline terminal versus the West Coast terminal. What if the West Coast terminal could influence the East Coast terminal? What if that individual terminal could then influence their colleagues' terminal? Essentially, the ripple effect or the domino effect could turn a negative into a positive, transforming the entire airline experience for both employees and passengers. Perhaps you're currently facing a negative event or situation. What solutions or ideas could you implement to flip the switch, making a sweeping turn on the negative domino effect into a potent positive one? In other words, in business, the idea is not to be held prisoner, so to speak, by any person, situation, event, or circumstance.

> *"But every company of the future is going to be in the business of exquisite care – which means quick turnaround time and convenience. To deliver exquisite care, you need an organization that coordinates well and listens well." ~ Fernando Flores."*

Addressing Inconsistencies with Culture

What if the leadership at the East Coast Terminal recognized the root constraint behind their employees' toxic, negative attitudes? Maybe you're currently navigating a human resource issue and are uncertain about the next steps. **Not doing anything sends the message that such behavior and culture are acceptable.** By avoiding the issue, everyone loses — the company, the employees, the customers, and the individual in question. Dodging the conflict might hinder or halt the domino effect at that specific juncture. Ask yourself: What are some practical ways to address that particular person or situation using people skills? The goal should be resolution, not punishment. How can you use powerful questions to realign that mindset with the business's core values? It might be helpful to revisit the original agreements, roles, and commitments made. Ensure you approach the situation professionally, without making it personal or questioning their motives.

Tips for Addressing Inconsistencies

1. Was the employee's role clearly defined?
2. Does the employer subcontractor understand clearly division, mission, and core values?
3. Has a Coaching Culture been established, meaning that feedback is "the breakfast of champions"?
4. Setting up a mechanism for feedback and growth opportunities for the team?
5. Establish a learning culture within your company.
6. Consider acknowledging healthy domino effects through your huddles, emails, newsletters, and whiteboards.
7. Giving weekly shout-outs for jobs well done.
8. Always address the individual privately.
9. Avoid gossip, criticism, and complaining.
10. Never make the inconsistency personal or judge their heart motives.

Application With Consistency

One of the simplest and most productive keys to success is consistency. When a leader is consistent, that in and of itself creates a domino effect. For example, consider the decision to walk a certain number of steps daily. This will have a domino effect not only physically over three months but will also cascade, influencing other areas of one's life. What could you consistently put into motion daily that creates a domino effect within, through, and outward, touching your customers? Watching actual dominos touch each other, they produce a rhythmic sound. Sounds attract people. One way to maintain consistency is to invite your team to focus on one domino a week, like fostering a culture of celebration. You might even take a risk by inviting them to agree on the next week's domino. Over time, these dominos are stacked, fostering the business rhythm synergistically.

1. How could you prepare your team for a consistent domino effect?
2. Where are the spaces that are too far apart to reach the next domino?
3. Scaling your brand — how could you position your current resources to foster a domino effect?

"Success is the sum of small efforts, repeated day in and day out."
~ Robert Collier.

Domino Effect With Habits

What if you're just one new habit away from achieving Synergistic Rhythm in your business? For example, consider the habit of washing the dishes after each meal. A pile of dishes in the sink can influence the peace in the home, subtly altering attitudes. If an attitude releases frustration or negativity, it can impact everyone in the home. Now, think about your team. What if you implemented one new habit every month for a year? What would be the ripple effect five years later? Consider aspects like how the phone is answered or how you greet a customer when they arrive for their appointment. The domino effect of consistently implementing the right habits each month can propel your business goals to significant growth.

Actions to Consider:

1. What one new habit could you implement this month?
2. During a huddle, ask the team what new habit they feel would fuel growth.
3. What habits would fuel a domino effect of business growth?

Take The First Step - 52 Weeks

The power of the domino effect holds significant potential for increasing your sales, profits, and market share awareness. Consider tracking your dominoes for fifty consecutive weeks and evaluating their effectiveness. Think about using and implementing dominoes that have a minimal cost but yield a high impact. Gathering feedback from your team and customers during this period can greatly fuel the domino effect. Remember, once all the dominoes are positioned and the first one is tipped, it will set in motion all the dominoes in its path. Your potential for massive growth might be just one domino away.

*"It's not what we do once in a while that shapes our lives.
It's what we do consistently." ~ Tony Robbins*

CHAPTER FOUR

The Vacuum Effect

The Vacuum

A vacuum draws opportunity; it's the opposite of repelling opportunity or people. The heart of rhythm draws people back to your business, culture, and people. Rhythm has a sound to it. It's like business culture — we can see it, hear it, and experience it. Culture is like the personality of an individual. There are many different aspects to their personality and their charisma.

"If you are working on something exciting that you really care about, you don't have to be pushed. The vision pulls you." ~ Steve Jobs

Many years ago, I had the distinct honor of building a 12,000 sq. ft. home with one of our companies. It was entered into our local Parade of Homes, and we were grateful to have won the premier award in our region that year. The home had three floors and 55 roof surfaces, offering spectacular open views. This home had a unique personality that continuously drew people from all over our region to see it.

"Alone, we can do so little; together, we can do so much." ~ Helen Keller

Momentum Has a Ripple Effect

Word started to spread in our region, drawing 15,000 adults to the home over ten days. One day, cars lined up a mile away, waiting to tour this residence. Our team was extraordinary, hosting so many guests consistently over the span of ten days. The police once told us we had to shut down because traffic was backed up for a mile. We thanked the officer for his service to our community, and he, understanding the positive impact on the community as a whole, assisted us with traffic flow. The remarkable thing was that none of us had ever experienced or seen anything like this before.

Rhythm Builds Awareness

We stepped into a Synergistic Rhythm that had been building over a one-year period, ready to host this many curious adults. This was all new territory for us. We drew from significant principles to sustain this thriving rhythm. To prepare the team, subcontractors, and vendors, we strategized intentionally around our systems, safety, culture, core values, and the hosting of all these viewers. Like waves in the ocean that build offshore, so did our business rhythm.

Intentionally Setting Context

A major key to our success was gathering the entire team in a conference room and working through schedules, potential supply issues, weather considerations, and how to interconnect all trades to build over the winter, aiming for 100% completion for judging. We encountered major adversities, surprises, and setbacks. Early on, we realized that everyone needed to grasp the bigger picture, the "why" behind our endeavors. They also needed assurance about the bright future and potential work for their companies.

The Conversation Built Rhythm

Our entire team sensed the uniqueness of this moment. There was a palpable alignment between us and our client. Collectively, we defined our job site culture, systems, and people dynamics. It felt like an orchestra producing a melody that resonated throughout our community. Our team became vision carriers, emphasizing the unique features and building applications, as well as our collective heart and culture. We believe our words and conversations shape realities. By being intentionally positive daily, we fostered a thriving culture. Embracing challenges and celebrating daily victories, we noticed a growing positive curiosity in the community.

Connection Over Coffee and Donuts

We recognized a vacuum was created, drawing enthusiasm and setting a high standard within our industry. One of the simple but profound ideas was how to build a bridge with the homeowner and all the tradespeople. To bridge this gap, we proposed to the homeowner the idea of serving coffee and donuts at 9:30 a.m. every day. Recognizing the potential value in this act of fostering connections, the homeowner agreed. This simple gesture enhanced the rapport between tradesmen and the homeowner, with workers drawn to the homeowner's appreciation for their diligent work. This organic initiative fostered connection and synergy among everyone involved in building this award-winning home. It leads us to the question: What single idea could you implement to foster synergy and connection between your customers and team?

"In nature, we never see anything isolated, but everything in connection with something else which is before it, besides it, under it, and over it."
~ Jonathan Wolfgang von Goethe

Feed the Wave of Momentum

Feeding the rhythm with intentional celebrations, ideas, and innovation allowed each tradesperson to share and express themselves during the 9:30 break. One day, the homeowner called and said, "The coffee and donuts are ready, but I'm not feeling my best; could you come pick them up?" This gesture touched all our hearts, showing that such care, honor, and respect was intentional. Despite the homeowner needing rest, the momentous rhythm and culture continued.

Culture Carriers

Your team and clients all yearn to be a part of something bigger than themselves. Cultivating that deeper reason with intention, no matter the size of the project, is crucial. Despite the challenges of winter and the adversity that sometimes accompanies building, we collectively maintained the rhythm. We all recognized the benefits this home brought to the local building industry and the community at large. Leading an orchestra, or any team, requires a vision carrier for your business. Achieving greatness, excellence, and gold medals doesn't happen by accident.

The Wave Will Carry

Think of surfers out in the ocean, on their boards, reading and feeling the waves. When they spot a promising wave, they commit to paddling and then standing up to ride the wave's vast energy. A skilled surfer can not only read the waves but also feel them as if they are one with the water.

1. How could you feel that connection in your business waters?
2. What one idea could you implement to have your team rally behind? What is your coffee and donuts question?
3. How could you foster the reason your business exists consistently?

The Power of Commitment

The concept of commitment could be a key to enhancing and expanding your business results. Let's delve into the power of commitment. Commitment can also create a magnetic pull, attracting like-mindedness and a unified focus to your ecosystem. When you hear the word "commitment," what comes to mind? Webster's dictionary defines commitment as: "an agreement or pledge to do something in the future, especially an engagement to assume a financial obligation at a future date." Now, consider the idea of next-level commitment. What might a renewed commitment to new habits, fresh perspectives, wealth mindsets, goals, personal growth, or a growth area in your business or life look like? As a leader, how could you demonstrate bold commitment to your team? Which commitment would help instill rhythm in your business?

Growing Greater Results

In the context of producing enhanced results, commitment essentially boils down to a decision stemming from personal responsibility because one has given one's word. A renowned coach once said that if you aim to achieve big things, you must make big commitments. What major commitment can you make to your business, team, systems, or culture? When you commit, how can you ensure that your team sees and believes in your dedication? Just as culture is contagious, the act of honoring commitments also spreads by example.

"Commitment is the foundation of great accomplishments."
~ Heidi Reeder

The Impact of Big Commitments

Making big commitments with a sense of honor can catalyze our actions, leading to significantly larger results. Consistently fulfilling commitments can challenge and overcome complacent mindsets. Making and following through on significant commitments can also combat a mindset of convenience that lacks grit and fortitude. Just as physical muscles grow with exercise, grit, and fortitude can be developed by sticking to commitments, even when faced with challenges. A firm commitment to one's word can overcome the lure of comfort, which often delays greatness. To nurture a habit of honoring commitments, consider maintaining a commitment journal and checking off tasks as they are completed.

"Most people fail not because of a lack of desire but because of a lack of commitment." *~ Vince Lombardi*

Elevating the Importance of Commitments

How can we elevate the importance of honoring commitments? Consider sharing your commitments with a trusted coach, mentor, or individual who will uphold a high standard, helping you excel and ensuring you achieve your goals. What major commitment can you make this week to enhance your business or a specific area of your life?

The Outcome of Significant Commitments

Let's delve into the potential outcomes of adhering to significant commitments. Firstly, what prevents many leaders from honoring their commitments? Could it be the fear of failure or a mindset that says, "I've failed at this before; why commit again?" Perhaps it's the fear of rejection? A way to navigate through the barrier of fear is through decisive action! Imagine deciding to take that first step on a walk; as you move, your body warms up, and energy emerges from the very act of moving. Many discover that as they take steps towards their purpose, it fuels their deepest passions.

"Commitment is what transforms a promise into a reality."
~ Abraham Lincoln

Here's the corrected paragraph:

Strengthening the Commitment Muscle

To develop the ability to make BIG commitments, start by setting and fulfilling smaller commitments. Take, for instance, the simple but significant act of KEEPING YOUR WORD REGARDING TIME. Most leaders who make major commitments inevitably face challenges along the way. For example, when driving to a vacation destination, isn't it common to encounter traffic jams, red lights, and rest stops? Yet, the anticipation of the vacation keeps them focused and resilient, ensuring they persevere.

Using TIME as an illustrative point, casual attitudes can undermine our commitment. When someone gets accustomed to tardiness, it can solidify into a habit deeply ingrained in their belief system. For a leader, punctuality is a basic way to show respect and value for others. Let's challenge ourselves: what if, for the next seven days, you committed to being punctual? Remember to account for unforeseen delays like rush hour or road accidents. By doing so, not only will you be on time, but you may even find yourself arriving early. Then, observe how this practice amplifies your appreciation for the principle of honoring commitments.

> *"If you aren't going all the way, why go at all?"*
> *~ Joe Namath*

Elevate Your Commitments

The act of making a commitment is elevated when shared with a mentor or coach. Consistently honoring these commitments can significantly enhance one's trustworthiness. In fact, trust in us grows when we consistently keep our word. The notion of honor is deeply intertwined with commitment. To honor is to treat someone with high esteem, recognizing their exceptional value. Conversely, to dishonor is to treat someone with disrespect or as if they are ordinary. Could it be that trust and honor within a company culture can flourish simply by maintaining the commitment to punctuality?

> *"Without commitment, nothing happens."*
> *~ T.D. Jakes*

Creating Urgency

Consider enhancing the principle of being on time by introducing an element of urgency. By raising the standard through urgency, we can catalyze desired outcomes. In essence, if you choose to complete a task within an hour, the combination of urgency and commitment can yield exponential results. Consider setting a goal with a firm commitment and then introduce a timeframe to add that element of urgency.

Fueling Commitment

Deepen your understanding of commitment by intertwining it with focused urgency, refining your action steps as you go. Picture a first responder dedicated to an emergency; their extensive training, combined with a passion for saving lives, enables them to act calmly under pressing time constraints. This is commitment channeled towards a larger purpose. Harness time as an ally, not an adversary. For instance, set commitments like "I pledge to lose 10 pounds by a specific date" or "I am committed to getting three new sales by a set date."

1. What is one commitment you can make to further develop your systems, culture, or team?
2. With whom could you share your commitments, someone who won't judge you but will uphold the standard for you?
3. What is that one significant, positive commitment you could embrace to shift your business development towards thriving growth?

"There's a difference between interest and commitment. When you're interested in doing something, you do it only when it's convenient. When you're committed to something, you accept no excuses; only results." ~ Kenneth Blanchard

Rhythm of System, People, and Culture

Does your business or organization struggle with consistent rhythm? Do you grapple with uncertainty on how to keep interconnected with the multiple moving parts? Given all the decisions to be made and elements to consider, you might wonder, "Where do I start?" Just as the Golden Gate Bridge relies on massive support pillars to maintain its structure and consistently fulfill its purpose, let's examine three interconnected pillars essential for sustaining and building a thriving business or organizational rhythm. The construction of the Golden Gate Bridge began with planning and engineering. How might you initiate a plan to foster Synergistic Rhythm in your current environment?

CHAPTER FIVE

Three Pillars of Business Rhythm

Three Pillars for Rhythm:

1.) System

2.) People

3.) Culture

1.) System: "A group of interacting, interrelated, or interdependent elements forming a complex whole." - American Heritage Dictionary

A system could be the interaction and interconnection of various parts of your business that collectively produce a result. To provide some examples, consider how ideas, information, innovation, employees, customers, brand, culture, finances, sales, products, and services all interact systematically to yield a specific outcome.

Evaluate your current systems. Which system has become ineffective? Which system can be tweaked to foster synergy among individuals and nurture a thriving culture? Let's consider a potential simple SYSTEMS action step:

System Awareness Action:

1. List your current systems that work.
2. How do the three pillars interact and interconnect within your business?
3. Which current systems are not working?

2.) People: This category encompasses employees, customers, subcontractors, associates, and even social media followers. Essentially, it includes every person internally within your business and every individual your business interacts with.

People Awareness Action:

1. What consistent, intentional plan is in place to foster personal growth?
2. What do customers experience when interacting with your team?
3. How would you describe the sense of belonging felt by your employees, team, or subcontractors?

3.) Culture: Culture is what we experience when we walk into a business. It's embodied by people, hinted at by the decor, and even suggested by the lighting and music. Culture can offer you an advantage over industry peers. While it encompasses the brand, it also goes beyond it. Your systems can also reflect your culture. It might also be described as the heart and soul of the business.

Culture Awareness Action:

1. Which culture currently embodies your vision, purpose, and mission?

2. What do employees or customers say about their experiences your company?

3. Which cultural attributes do you want to define your business?

In the upcoming blogs, we will delve deeper into each individual pillar. Each post aims to foster action, feedback, and ideas to establish and synchronize each pillar for enhanced rhythm.

Intentional Rhythm

For a business to maintain a thriving ecosystem, systematic intention is essential. Launching, growing, and sustaining a business can often feel overwhelming and intricate. Let's consider a four-part approach to unify every facet of Systems, People, and Culture. Let's call this P.D.C.A.:

- **PLAN** Rhythm
- **DO** Rhythm
- **CHECK** Rhythm
- **ADJUST** Rhythm

Plan Rhythm

Purposeful planning can yield impressive results! Consider a harmonious synergy with many components of your plan operating in unison. Sports teams rely on playbooks for strategy. What if you had a playbook or, better yet, a "plan book"? How does this plan manage existing operations? How does it stimulate new growth? Every business area should be methodically planned. When each segment is intentionally interconnected, a rhythm emerges that propels the plan forward.

Do Rhythm

Achieving anything noteworthy requires consistent action. Let's call this "Doing Rhythm." In essence, it's a commitment to intentional actions derived from the initial plan. Such action is bolstered by a rhythm of habits operating synergistically. A professional football player's regimen involves practice, playbook reviews, and engagement both on and off the field. This is all doing rhythm. Rhythm is active, not stationary.

Check Rhythm

After devising and implementing a plan, it's crucial to check the plan. Continual action without periodic evaluations or feedback can be detrimental, stunting growth or leading to considerable losses. Anything measurable can provide feedback, allowing for necessary adjustments and adaptations to realign with the intended rhythm. On the people side of the business, regular feedback can foster and drive a dynamic growth rhythm. Roles for your team can be mapped out, assessed, and fine-tuned.

Adjust Rhythm

Much like a football team marching down the field, constant adjustments based on feedback are essential. A great coach has a list of plays and has to always be ready to adjust and pivot to plays that have been practiced. The coach is always gauging the team's momentum. Sustaining the rhythm requires the concerted awareness of the entire squad. During gusty conditions, a flag stands out most prominently. Similarly, it can pivot on its pole with changing winds, displaying its vibrant colors.

"The most difficult thing is the decision to act; the rest is merely tenacity." ~ *Amelia Earhart*

Potter's Wheel

Sculpting with skill requires a harmonious bond between the clay and the revolving rhythm of the potter's wheel. Without the hands-on manipulation of the clay, there's no deliberate molding or reshaping. The wheel's cadence, combined with a heartfelt connection to the clay, creates an avenue for crafting extraordinary masterpieces. How are you molding your business? I once conversed with a sculptor who mentioned that clay undergoes numerous stages before it's ready for the kiln. Consider giving your team the freedom to sculpt during the process, fostering patience and allowing a masterpiece to emerge.

Reshaping Your Rhythm

If you pause to reflect on your tangible interaction with your business, people, and systems, how are you guiding them to embody the business's vision? An adept potter occasionally feels an imperfection and readjusts the clay into an even more refined work of art. Modifying your current rhythm doesn't signify failure; it signifies the creation of a masterpiece.

The Heart of The Potter

True masterpieces are shaped from the heart, not mere logic. When there's a transition from the head to the heart in your business rhythm, incredible business artworks are showcased to the world. This intuitive expertise becomes evident to onlookers. Your rhythm emanates from intellectual principles and the palpable heart and soul of your business.

P.D.C.A.

Plan: *Execute* the plan with the intent to create systems. Catalog your current functioning systems. Exercise patience throughout the process, from A to Z. Key Point: Illuminate the reason behind each existing and new system. Always aim for simplicity in systems.

Do: *Act* on the plan. Once the plan is honed and consensus is reached, execute it for a specific duration. Remember, when introducing new plans, it's essential for your team to feel involved. Welcome their feedback and insights.

Check: *Evaluate* the plan. Solicit feedback. Establish metrics to gauge the results and efficacy of each strategy. How does your course of action intertwine with and influence other sectors of your business? Is it fostering rhythm?

Adjust: *Modify* the plan to optimize a thriving rhythm. What's effective? What isn't? Engage your team and customers in the feedback loop. Much like a car on a highway requires adjustments to stay within the lanes, similarly, ensure your plans are steering your business correctly. Avoid the pitfall of a fixed mindset that resists change. Such a stance can be detrimental to your business's success.

> *"Be clear about your goal, but be flexible about the*
> *process of achieving it."* ~ *Brian Tracy*

Three Pillars for Rhythm:

1.) System

2.) People

3.) Culture

Systems: Types of Possible Systems:

1. **Product or Service Systems:** Your manufacturing systems/processes, installation of goods supplied, and how the service is rendered.

2. **Information Systems**: All data stored/shared with team and customers, purchasing, inventory, customer lead tracking, and communication system.

3. **Culture Management Systems:** The branding, language communicated, colors on print, decor, and even dress code.

4. **People Development Systems:** Weekly huddles, coaching, leadership development, team trainings, sales training, and customer service training.

5. **Marketing Systems:** Sales systems, sales training, social media content system, customer referral process, branding, language, dress code, vehicles, and anything that customers may see, hear, or experience.

6. **Financial Systems:** Measure cost, budgets, purchase orders, estimation, manage chart of accounts, accounts payable, accounts receivable, employee cost, subcontractors, taxes, all things financial put into systems. Remember, haste makes waste.

7. **Research and Development:** Having a system that allows growth with both existing and future products and services. Empower your team to create solutions.

"Functional things cannot thrive in dysfunctional systems."
~ Hendrith Smith, CEO of Mayflower Plymouth

People: Employees, customers, subcontractors, associates, and even social media. Basically, every person internally within your business and every person with whom your business comes in contact.

"The growth and development of people is the highest
calling of leadership." ~ Harvey Firestone

Let's Unpack Some Applications to Grow Your PEOPLE Capacity:

1. As a leader, ask: "How does each person on my team interconnect, upholding the systems and the culture?"
2. Explore: "What is our customers' experience with our employees and subcontractors?"

Note: These keys can apply to either your Team or your Customers.

Clearly Communicated Roles

1. Does each person clearly know their role? Are the roles in writing to revisit?
2. Have a system for intentional benchmarking of their growth and results in their roles.
3. Communicate expectations with their role and the interaction with systems and culture.
4. Clearly define goals and objectives with each employee or subcontractor.

Key: Inspiration Before Information! It's important for people to understand the why.

Importance of Clarity: Understanding versus Misunderstanding:

1. In the context of **RHYTHM**, does every teammate know how they interconnect with each other?

2. Feedback is not punishment. Help each person understand your process for feedback.

3. Are all expectations clearly communicated? Uncommunicated expectations foster judgments that produce unnecessary conflicts and offenses.

4. If things are already in motion, consider initiating a time to inspire, share vision, and create clarity with roles and systems. Then, outline what you agreed on and ask them for feedback.

5. Write down what was communicated. Review again. Create the agreement. Then, revisit to avoid broken agreements.

Dealing with Conflict:

1. In the simplest way, keep all conflict about Broken Agreements and not about judging their heart motives.

2. The art of solving conflicts is the ability to create awareness around broken agreements and then reestablish that which was mutually agreed upon.

   Tip: Give up your right to be right. Avoid taking it personally.

3. Conflict in and of itself is a form of feedback.

4. To help facilitate an understanding of rhythm, consider creating a clear understanding through written agreements, then review, having them repeat back what they are hearing.

Tip: Whatever is tolerated consistently will eventually become culture.

5. The art of mutually updating agreements: At times, an agreement may need to be updated or adjusted. You may say, "I would value it if we could explore a win-win and renegotiate our agreement."

Teamwork Through Collaboration:

"Teamwork is the ability to work together toward a common vision."
~ Dale Carnegie

1. Consider short daily huddles as celebrating wins.
2. Ask your team for feedback: What is working? What is not working?
3. Possibly monthly idea exchange! Works well with food in a fun, positive environment, mining for golden ideas.
4. **Avoid 3 Cs:** Complaining, criticizing, and condescending. These three attitudes are like acid. They will erode and undermine your business rhythm.

What is your people growth plan?

1. Be intentional about investing in your team and customer experience.
2. Remember: thriving leaders attract more thriving people.

"People don't care how much you know until they know how much you care." ~ Theodore Roosevelt

Importance of Coaching: "I absolutely believe that people, unless coached, never reach their maximum capabilities." ~ Bob Nardelli

"A great leader inspires people to have confidence in themselves."
~ Eleanor Roosevelt

Recap: Three Pillars for Rhythm:

1.) System

2.) People

3.) Culture

Importance of CULTURE sustaining a thriving Rhythm

"Culture is simply a shared way of doing something with a passion."
~ Brian Chesky, Co-Founder, CEO, Airbnb

Culture:

Culture is what we all experience when walking into a business. It embodies the attitudes and core values shared by everyone. This is evident not just in the people but also in the decor, lighting, and even the music. Culture can give your business an edge over industry peers. While it includes the brand, it goes beyond just that. Even your systems can be representative of your culture. Culture could also be described as the heart and soul of the business. Remember, whatever is tolerated will eventually become the culture.

Duplication of Culture:

I recently spoke with a manager from a large coffee company. He said, "Ed, I'm struggling to reproduce our culture in other stores." As you cultivate a culture that resonates with your business, consider its reproducibility. What aspects can be duplicated in other locations or settings? It might be helpful to keep a journal or even consult an expert who specializes in establishing and reproducing culture.

Culture Awareness:

1. What CULTURE is currently carrying your vision, purpose, and mission?
2. What do employees or customers say about their experience with your company?
3. What are the core values carrying your business?

What Are the Core Values?

Think of core values as akin to driving a vehicle on the right side of the highway. Awareness of core values provides constant feedback, ensuring safe travel while delivering a product or service to its destination. Core values define both our "yes" and our "no." They can be likened to the lanes in a bowling alley, helping to guide our direction. Another analogy is to think of them as pistons in an engine, all working together in a rhythmic harmony.

> *"Company Culture is the product of a company's values, expectations and environment." ~ Courtney Chapman, Product Manager, Rubicon Project*

Culture Carries Vision

Whenever you think of a thriving business, there's always an underlying element that might not be immediately noticeable. If you frequent a business, what is it that sets it apart? How can you transform a business or organization that's merely surviving? What single step can you take now to shift from merely surviving to genuinely thriving? Let's delve into a crucial component of a prosperous business.

"Culture eats strategy for breakfast." ~ Peter Drucker

"Why is culture so important to a business? Here is a simple way to frame it. The stronger the culture, the less corporate process a company needs. When the culture is strong, you can trust everyone to do the right thing." ~ Brian Chesky, CEO, Airbnb

Knowing and Defining Your Culture

A straightforward way to establish your culture is to define it:

- What five core values do you want to embody in your culture? Think of innovative ways for both you and your team to embody these core values.
- Encourage your team to discuss them amongst themselves.
- Prompt them to internalize the core values, emphasizing the experience and manifestation of those values rather than just the words.

To truly understand the culture, it's crucial to recognize how the culture propels the vision.

Build With a Culture Blueprint

Without a robust, deliberate culture, your vision will stall in the long run! You might have come across the saying, "If it's to be, it's up to me." Another resonant phrase goes, "All ships rise and fall on leadership." For culture to truly thrive, all leaders must champion it daily and intentionally!

"When you hand good people possibility, they do great things."
~ Biz Stone

Questions to Consider

1. What uniquely sets you apart?
2. What could define you differently from other businesses like you in your market region?
3. What does it look like when you know everything is working in harmony?

Two Ways Culture is Formed:

1. Culture forms unintentionally over time. Whether good or bad, whatever is tolerated will eventually become the culture.
2. The best cultures are established through purposeful intention.

Culture Has an Attitude:

Everything embodies a culture. Culture reflects the attitudes, behaviors, and core values understood and shared by a group of people. Whatever a business leader allows will eventually manifest in the culture.

1. Celebrate with your team when you observe the desired culture in action.
2. Regularly remind the team about the culture's components.
3. Continually inspire them about the "why" behind each cultural attribute. Without the "why," it just becomes more information and noise.

"The culture of a workplace – an organization's values, norms, and practices – has a huge impact on our happiness and success."
~ Adam Grant

The Domino Effect

In Chapter Three, we spent some time on the power of the domino effect. We all have seen when we touch one domino how many begin to cascade. Think for a moment about how you could start with one core value or attribute and put that in motion. How could you inspire and touch the hearts and minds of your team like a domino effect? How could you carry this core value into your customer experience? I want to encourage you not to wait until everything is perfect with all the marketing and four-color brochures. Culture flows out of a heart attitude and permeates every part of the business. Yes, every aspect of your business carries culture, unknowingly or knowingly.

"Our secret weapon for building the best culture is open and honest feedback." ~ Gina Lau

Actions to Consider

1. Inspire your sphere of relationships with the WHY behind your culture.
2. Since language forms and cultivates culture, what words and language can you use to continually paint culture? What atmosphere can you create with culture?
3. Celebrating WINS on the team will FEED and FUEL passion behind the day-to-day activities.
4. Invite your teams to create an active and alive experience.
5. Celebrating culture going in the right direction will CONNECT the culture to their hearts.

"Corporate culture is the only sustainable competitive advantage that is completely within the control of the entrepreneur. Develop a strong corporate culture first and foremost." ~ David Cummings, Co-Founder of Pardot

Creating Core Values:

1. What are five to eight CORE VALUES for your business or organization?
2. Collaborate with your team. Ask for their feedback on what the vision carries. What do they hear from repeat and satisfied customers?
3. It's important to define each core value in your own words. The mistake many make is that they're operating with someone else's core values.
4. List and revisit them a few times a month until the core values and definition create the lines on the highway, giving culture its guidelines. Core Values should bring focus, clarity, and enthusiasm.

Core Values Applied:

1. Be intentional about what you're building by integrating the Core Values into every aspect of your business. Think of a builder with a specific set of plans.
2. Empower your team to integrate each core value within their team and into customer service.
3. During your team huddles, share wins of how the core values showed up on the team and in customer service. Acknowledge and reward how the core values are applied, fostered, and integrated into your systems. Honor and celebrate creativity and initiative.
4. Does your team know the core values?

Key: Inspire the why behind each core value. Share the heart behind each core value.

Model the Culture:

1. **BECOME and BE** the culture you desire.
2. **LIVE and LEARN** the culture to reflect.
3. Culture is caught more than taught.

CULTURE carries RHYTHM:

> *"Everyone on the team plays an equal role. My role is to create the wave, and everyone on our team keeps the wave going."*
> *~ William Wang, Founder, Vizio*

Think of CULTURE like the waves in the ocean carrying the surfer or like the high tide taking every boat higher because it's in the water. Going back to the three parts, Systems, People, and Culture. We invite you to start with your five to eight core values and practice integrating them into the day-to-day rhythm of your company or organization. Remember to inspire your team and avoid pushing your team. People respond and stay for the long haul through being empowered.

> *"Performance more often comes down to a cultural challenge, rather than simply a technical one."* *~ Lara Hogan, Senior Engineering Manager of Performance, Etsy*

Action Awareness:

Take inventory of where your culture is at now. Then 30/60/90/120 days from now, benchmark where your culture is at. Ask, are the core values becoming part of conversations and feedback from customers?

Culture Perspectives:

1. *"Customers will never love a company until the employees love it first." ~ Simon Sinek, author, Start with Why*

2. *"There's no magic formula for great company culture. The key is just to treat your staff how you would like to be treated." ~ Richard Branson, Founder, Virgin Group*

3. *"Corporate culture is the only sustainable competitive advantage that is completely within the control of the entrepreneur." ~ David Cummings, Co-Founder*

CHAPTER SIX

Honoring Rhythm

Biological Circadian Rhythm

What can we learn from our biological circadian rhythm to grow a synergistic business rhythm? First, our body has a built-in rhythm to maintain thriving health. Think of it like an internal built-in master clock located in the brain that has built-in settings to activate thriving body processes. Our biological systems are all interconnected to optimize thriving health.

For example, our sleep pattern is important to our circadian rhythm. Our body will give us feedback when we are not getting consistent sleep. When I was a teenager, I didn't truly understand the high value of consistent sleep patterns. Therefore, I would drink and eat more sugars to compensate, only to find myself out of sync with my natural circadian rhythm.

Wellness Has a Rhythm

Learning from our extraordinary physical biology, the body always gives us feedback. Have you ever heard the term "listen to your body"? What they mean is that our body gives us indicators to make adjustments and stay in the rhythm or the wellness lane. When visiting the doctor for a physical, what are some of the first things they do? They take various measurements.

For example, your pulse, blood pressure, temperature, height, weight, check flexibility, check lymphatic systems, look inside ears and mouth. In other words, the doctors have a systematic approach to get feedback from our biology and then ask a series of questions. Then, the doctor gives recommendations: pivot, adjust, and make lifestyle changes. What if the same intentional approach was implemented within your business to make the adjustment?

Feedback is The Breakfast for Champions

One way to delay business growth and development is avoiding feedback and measuring to acquire the right data and feedback. Like the human body, it's dynamic, full of potential and is truly extraordinary! Many have been studying the human body for thousands of years. Avoiding making adjustments can be very costly. Ask yourself, if this was resolved/solved, how would it influence your business or life in a positive way?

"It takes humility to seek feedback. It takes wisdom to understand it, analyze it, and appropriately act on it." ~ *Stephen Covey*

Rhythm is a Living Organism

Think of your business as a living organism. It has a personality, a heart, core value standards, and people with their own passions and personalities. While we can implement organizational systems, your business, as an organism, thrives when the heart of the matter is treasured, fed, and nurtured. Avoidance is never healthy. There is a difference between recognizing an opportunity or conflict and searching for the best solution. In other words, learning the art of not being reactive but leading well by being proactive. Think of how important a few simple adjustments can make the journey of thriving growth a pleasant experience!

Honoring Your Rhythm

Let's apply the principle of circadian rhythm to various facets of our business. Leaders who choose to steer the business in sync with its rhythm will attract more sales, longer customer retention, higher profits, and lower costs. Efficiency and effectiveness can be significant positive outcomes when steering the business into its rhythm. Maybe you've heard the rumble strips while driving, warning that the vehicle needs to be steered back on course. Honoring your business's rhythm will help sustain thriving growth.

Intentional Listening

Just like our physical bodies, we can avoid listening to them. However, eventually, they will remind us to step back into rhythm, or they will enforce some rest. Our business operates similarly. This relates back to our systems, people, and culture, incorporating dashboard lights, much like in a vehicle, to provide feedback. We might refer to this as being intentional. Consider the power of active listening: understanding before speaking.

Explore Business Rhythm Systems

To steer a ship, a captain relies on its instruments. Ask yourself how you could lay out a simple but consistent way to get feedback from your business to make a calculated choice based on feedback. Below is a partial list of potential benchmarks to factor in your thriving rhythm. Think of non-tangibles to put on the list. Business rhythm goes way beyond the numbers.

Business Diagnostics

When a person purchases a new vehicle, they have a systematic diagnostic protocol from the manufacturer that keeps the vehicle in optimal performance. Our heart with this book is to create awareness of what is possible in operating a business with Synergistic Rhythm. The manufacturer of that vehicle has their 50-100 point checklist. They have their recommendation for maximum vehicle life. What if it's possible to custom-tailor your very own diagnostic feedback checklist to create ongoing optimal rhythm? A constant business feedback mechanism. There are tangible and intangible feedback opportunities.

Business Benchmarks To Measure For Feedback:

- System
- People
- Culture
- Core Values
- Sales
- Lead Flow
- Customer Service
- Employee Retention
- Testimonials
- 5 Star reviews
- Overall Team Attitudes
- Volunteers For Special Projects
- Cash Flow
- Profits
- Referrals
- Technology Engagement
- Social Media Engagement

- Overhead
- Accounts Payables
- Accounts Receivables
- Attendance To Offsite Events
- New Systems
- Training Attendance
- Huddle Feedback
- Is Culture Life-Giving
- Willingness For the Team To Grow And Learn
- How Are The Core Values Being Sustained
- New growth
- Team synergy

The Huddle Concept

Many sports teams have huddles to empower, equip, adjust, call plays, pivot, and rotate teammates, to name a few. To steer your business vision into Synergistic Rhythm, consider setting up consistent huddles daily, weekly, monthly, quarterly, and even yearly. Remember vision leaks, being intentional as a leader to have huddles, even smaller team huddles that all interconnect. Building an interconnected business culture creates awareness of all teams and allows for sharpening skills.

Vision Leaks

Like a swimming pool in the hot sun, the water will evaporate. Pools have a built-in mechanism to keep water at a particular level. Keeping the water level at a certain level allows the water filtration to work properly. Vision is a lot like that. In the heat of the day, the daily grind, so to speak, people can sometimes forget the why, the vision, which can lead teams in a more negative or fault-finding bent. We, as leaders, have a great opportunity to empower other leaders by nurturing and inspiring the bigger vision. Think of fun, creative ways of building vision, like putting a puzzle together—celebrating each step that someone takes toward the vision!

Whale Done

The book *Whale Done!* by Ken Blanchard has a powerful illustration of celebrating team and employee behavior going in the right direction. In other words, with daily awareness, celebrate someone on your team who is moving the company vision in the right direction. Perhaps it's through a review, a satisfied customer, or an internal process that impacts everyone. Make a big deal in a positive way about actions taken by your team that move the business into a Synergistic Rhythm. This will create dynamic team synergy and help improve retention. All employees become great vision carriers. This is a creative way to begin steering your new business culture.

Find Your Dream Team

One of the challenges in business can be the transition season of launching new ideas, systems, and those waves of growth. Owning a business is not for the faint of heart. To maintain a healthy rhythm, one thing to consider is going it alone is not effective long term.

Reflection

I can remember falling asleep at my desk night after night, trying to finish an estimate for our building company. I would wake up early to go to the job site during the day and then work on the business at every possible moment: at lunch, during breaks, and in the evening hours. When I first started in business, the prevailing mindset was to do as much as you could on your own. The thought of growing our team through interns never even crossed our minds. I want to encourage you to, as quickly as possible, enlist others around you — talented individuals with great skills. Delegate to them, empower them, train them, and add value to their roles to help steer the vision, all while regaining the time that keeps you in your lane!

Concept of Intern

Create so much value in what you do that others are drawn to your vision and desire to grow with you! Awareness is key. Keep sharing what you're doing in your business on social media and through emails. This will share your vision, attracting other like-minded leaders to you. Many people today possess diverse skill sets that can be creatively applied. You might think, *Well, we have no budget for hiring.* I personally volunteered for almost five years with a company, acquiring life-changing coaching and facilitation skills that have deeply enriched my life. Raise awareness and provide opportunities for others to envision themselves interning at your company. Consider serving in areas where you aim to grow and expand.

> *"It is literally true that you can succeed best and quickest by helping others to succeed." ~ Napoleon Hill.*

One Phone Call

Like a sail catching the wind, one day, we received a call from a subcontractor seeking a solution for a challenge faced by his customer. This call resulted in over three years of work on a 20,000 sq. ft. premier estate. In order to sustain and nurture our Synergistic Rhythm, we chose to pivot quickly to accommodate this next level of business growth.

To add to the challenge, this project was almost two hours away. How prepared are you for next-level growth? Success is never convenient, and neither is winning gold medals! With a firm commitment, our team pivoted, managing growth in two locations simultaneously. What are you putting in place today to attract future opportunities to your company? It's worth noting that this referral stemmed from relationships and giving back to another company, which ultimately led to that transformative phone call.

A Heart of Contribution

The heart of business is to serve and make contributions to others, elevating their influence and lifting those around them, ultimately bettering the world. Reflect for a moment on interns: how can your company amplify its commitment to service? How can you cultivate a legacy mindset within your internal and external teams? This 20,000 sq. ft. estate opportunity arose not just from a relationship but also from our decision to volunteer framing labor to help launch a person's millwork business. It was a gesture stemming from a genuine desire to see another's dream grow and thrive. When a business shines as a beacon of positivity and hope, it attracts excellence. The world is in search of uplifting, life-affirming work cultures. People truly value feeling appreciated!

Power of Thank You

Even a simple "thank you" can transform a person and foster a culture that encourages others to persevere. When I was young, I worked on an Amish farm. Though I wasn't Amish, I cherished working there almost every day. It instilled in me valuable attributes and skills. As a young boy and teenager, I would eagerly wait at the end of the day on my orange three-speed banana seat bike for the Amish farmer.

Marinating in the Thank You

Night after night, he would approach me as I sat there and simply say, "Garner, thanks for all your help today! You did a great job!" Those positive words resonated deeply with me. He was unaware that, during that period, I was bullied in school for four straight years. His words gave me the hope and strength to persevere. As a business owner, your words and the culture they foster can shape not only your business environment but may also provide someone the hope and encouragement they need to continue and not give up. That embodies a true heart of contribution. The Amish farm where I had the privilege of working operated with Synergistic Rhythm, driven by distinct core values. We consistently achieved growth, connection, culture, people-centric values, systems, and results month after month, year after year.

CHAPTER SEVEN

Trusting Your Instruments

Defining Doldrums

There is a nautical term called "doldrums." The doldrums refer to an area near the equator where there's a gap between the winds from the north and the winds from the south. Many years ago, if sailors were riding the momentum of the trade winds and veered off course, they might find themselves in this windless region, waiting in stagnation for the winds to pick up again. In business or life, what actions can we take when we find ourselves in such "doldrums"? Let's delve deeper into potential solutions to navigate out of these stagnant periods!

Newton's First Law (Law of Inertia)

Newton's First Law of Motion, in basic terms, states, "An object at rest will forever stay at rest, as long as there is not a force internally or externally that moves it." Think for a moment of a parked vehicle; it will remain parked unless some internal or external force moves it. The reality is that the object will remain at rest forever unless it's moved. This is a simple snapshot of being in a doldrum without any active, intentional movement or momentum!

Perhaps you're asking, "What are some warning signs to be aware of?" Maybe you feel trapped and are wondering how to break free. Do you notice recurring patterns where you feel stuck, as if in a doldrum? We will delve deeper into ideas and inspiration to help you grow and take decisive action.

"I never worry about action, but only inaction."
~ Winston Churchill

Resistance To Change

Many times, resistance to change, growth, or new ideals can look and feel like inertia. Even resistance to teammates or resistance to new opportunities can feel like a doldrum. I heard a term many years ago: ***"What We Resist Will Persist!"*** ~ Unknown. What is the resistance in your business or life where you can take the first step towards exploring solutions? What roadblock, competing commitment, or mindset could be delaying movement or momentum? Is there resistance around that sales call? That next growth idea? That unresolved conflict? Embracing that new growth habit? Take a moment and ask, "Is there a reoccurring mindset or habit pattern that seems to manifest when growth or change starts to take place?" Make a list of what you may be resisting and flip the switch, listing positive solutions beside it!

"Let us not be surprised when we have to face difficulties. When the wind blows hard on a tree, the roots stretch and grow the stronger, Let it be so with us. Let us not be weaklings, yielding to every wind that blows, but strong in spirit to resist." ~ Amy Carmichael

What Are Your Navigation Instruments?

We might ask, "Are our feelings and emotions truly reflective of our destiny?" A sailor cannot rely on their feelings and emotions during a storm. In navigating uncertain waters, the sailor must trust their instruments and compass to weather the storm. Without correctly steering into the waves, the sailboat could capsize. What tools can you employ to chart a successful course and avoid the doldrums? What consistent growth habits can you implement over the next three months?

Navigating the Fog

Many years ago, I was about 30 miles out in the ocean on a fishing boat. On the way back, a sudden heavy and dense fog settled in over the water. We could barely see past the edge of our fishing boat. Personally, I was a bit unsettled until I looked into our captain's eyes! For one hour, with a smile, our captain continued motoring through the fog, simultaneously balancing his thermos of coffee! He exuded confidence that he had done this before!

Trusting Your Instruments

The result of trusting his instruments and his ability to navigate through the fog was that he docked our boat perfectly at the pier. I asked him, "You smiled the whole time, sipping your coffee. How did you do that?"

He replied, "I trusted my instruments, not my feelings. The fog can play tricks on your mind."

I realized the importance of being around other captains who know how to navigate through the fog!

A Few Tips for Overcoming The Fog of Doldrums:

1. **Take Action Today**: Take steps forward in any area of life or business! This activates motion! Take that first step: make one call, call a client and thank them, read your goals, and look at your dream board. In other words, what one thing could you do to take action today?

2. **Phone a Friend**: Ask them to remind you of your purpose, vision, mission, or identity! Be vulnerable with where you're at, and they will pour encouragement into you! Isolation is a doldrum trap!

3. **Trust Your Instruments**: A few basic instruments:

A). Your core values.

B). Your team.

C). Read your vision, purpose, and mission.

D). Measure your numbers and finances. Avoidance will feed the doldrums.

4. **Gratitude**: Take out a pen and list what you are grateful for. Like walking, taking the first step of action begins to fill your sail and move the sailboat. Gratitude is a powerful instrument to not take the bait of Entitlement or Offense. Both of these will send a person into the doldrums.

5. **Read a Rainy Day Note:** Read a note from a customer, client, or friend. Go through and read cards, texts, and kind words! Read your why, mission, and purpose!

6. **Speak Your Goals Out Loud**: Speaking positive life into your goals, vision, business, and team begins to fill the heart with a wind of inspiration. Remember, our words form worlds!

7. **Focus – Celebrate WINS**: Write your daily WINS! Focus on the wins in your conversations. Highlight and celebrate things going well. Focus on what is working! What are the positives within your team? Write a WINS list!

> *"Determine that the thing....shall be done, and then [you] shall find the way." ~ Abraham Lincoln*

The Opportunity in the Stretch

Think for a moment: during the Great Depression, there was a vision to build the Empire State Building. For many, it was a stretch, but this vision fueled hope and vision! If you have ever driven across the Golden Gate Bridge, I am sure there was a captivated wonder and respect! I can remember crossing the Golden Gate Bridge for the first time and thinking, I am crossing to the other side on what was once a vision, now a reality! A vision that requires brilliant collaboration will stretch even the brightest engineers, builders, and many others to see it become a reality!

Vision Breaks Old Barriers

Think of Roger Bannister, the runner who decided one day to break the four-minute mile. Doctors believed if a person ran that fast, their heart would explode. Roger's vision fueled him to break the record! The four-minute mile barrier was broken many times the next year because Roger had shown them it was possible. Does your vision stretch you in a positive way? Do your circumstances dictate your vision, or does your vision tell your circumstances what the purposeful outcome is going to be?

Stretching Produces Flexibility

If you have ever played sports, a good coach always emphasizes stretching to stay flexible to help avoid injuries. How many of you enjoy exercising? Do you see being stretched in business is like a new physical workout? Stretching can take you and your organization into new territory, skills, and opportunity. Do you find yourself avoiding the pain in the stretch? After a good workout, most people experience more energy! What could be new or unique that you could do to stretch you and cause you to expand?

"Your only limitations are those you set up in your mind, or permit others to set up for you." ~ Og Mandino

Discoveries from 100 Days of Push-ups

Adding One A Day

In August of 2021, I had this personal vision to do one hundred push-ups in a hundred days, starting with one, then each consecutive day, adding one push-up for one hundred days! To elevate my commitment, I shared this vision with those around me. This was part of a continuation of my personal wellness growth. Push-ups have been something I was avoiding for years due to fear of hurting my right shoulder again. Explore that deep business vision you carry.

"Our limitations and success will be based, most often, on your own expectations for ourselves. What the mind dwells upon, the body acts upon." ~Denis Waitley

Surrounding Your Intention

The push-ups began with one on August 9th, then the next day, I did two, the third day, I did three. On day ten, I began to experience minor pain and had some doubts. I noticed resistance in my beliefs. However, I surrounded my intention with stretching, breathing, and visualizing the completion of 100 push-ups. The pain acted like a dashboard light, prompting me to incorporate various stretches, breathing exercises, and preparation techniques.

Overcoming Limitations

On day one hundred, I remember doing 50 push-ups, then lying on my back, stretching, breathing, and visualizing the finish line. Although my physical body felt like it was hitting a wall, I could visualize the ribbon at the finish line in my mind. I listened to inspirational music, which filled the atmosphere. Then, with determination, despite my arms resisting the bend, a renewed strength surged through my mind, will, and body. I focused on the vision, ignoring the pain. With deep breaths and my eyes closed, a surge of strength filled me. I managed to complete one hundred push-ups. What would victory over one limiting mindset look like?

CHAPTER EIGHT

Overcoming Rhythm Limitations

Vision Fuels Focus

The vision of a toned body fueled my commitment. On the hundredth day, my heart was racing with expectation and joy! Despite facing physical pain in areas of my body over the one hundred days, the commitment to the vision fueled me to finish! The results were so invigorating that I have continued to work out every day since August 9th!

Discoveries

1. Overcome limiting mindsets with supporting daily habits.
2. When resistance arises, keep stretching.
3. Raise the level of intention by committing to a coach, mentor, and friends.
4. You were born for greatness, not apathy.
5. One area of growth influences other areas of growth.
6. What is the underlying "why" behind your next big agreement?
7. What would be possible to break new growth records?
8. Overcome limiting mindsets with supporting daily habits.
9. When resistance arises, keep stretching.

10. Raise the level of intention by committing to a coach, mentor, and friends.
11. You were born for greatness, not apathy.
12. One area of growth influences other areas of growth.
13. What is the underlying "why" behind your next big agreement?
14. What would be possible to break new growth records?

"Don't limit yourself. Many people limit themselves to what they think they can do. You can go as far as your mind lets you. What you believe, remember, you can achieve." ~Mary Kay Ash

Benefits from Overcoming

I realized through the one hundred days of stretching that my lower back did not hurt at all! I am experiencing more energy and many other physical benefits. This was a stretch for sure, but I am so grateful for the discoveries and results. The vision stretched me to do what I had never accomplished before! What could you step into the next one hundred days, when completed, would advance your life, business, and organization forward? How can you feed your rhythm, overcoming limiting beliefs or mindsets? I am personally grateful to have maintained this habit every day for two solid years. It has influenced every area of my life.

What If Your Mirror Could Read Your Thinking?

Think about how you view yourself when you're looking in the mirror. What would your mirror reflect if it could read your thinking? What would you reflect if new habits supported a brand new mental movie? Your mind is like soil; it will return what is planted. Napoleon Hill said, "Any idea, plan or purpose may be placed in the mind through repetition of thought." We can sharpen our minds through repetition and daily habits of seeing and listening to the right data. No matter where you are, you can take decisive action today to begin transforming your life by changing what goes into your mind.

Gauges For Feedback

Our vehicles have gauges to provide us with constant feedback. The other day, a light flashed, "check coolant." I immediately turned off my engine. After waiting ten minutes, I drove a mile down the road to a mechanic who informed me that there were no leaks, but the coolant was low. He mentioned that whoever had flushed out the system hadn't filled it up completely. What if I hadn't taken decisive action? What if I had thought, *SOMEDAY, I'll get around to it*? The word "someday" means "at an indefinite time in the future." Procrastinating to "someday" could have been much more costly than a simple, free coolant "top off."

1. Write down areas where you need to "top off" your mental reservoir.
2. What mental gauges could you set up to give you feedback?
3. What process could you set up before you overheat your mind's engine?

Mental Toughness

Think of the body: we can tone it, shape it, and energize it with consistent workouts. We can choose to strengthen our minds on how we react to an event. The meaning we attach to each event will influence our mental perspective, which influences our emotions, attitudes, and choices.

"Growth is a great separator for those to succeed and those that don't."
~ John Maxwell

Fight, Flight, or Fright

Which of these reactions surfaces within you when you encounter an adversity similar to a previous one? You might have heard the term: **"Fight, Flight, or Fright."** For instance, when you hear the word **"CONFLICT!"** what is your initial response? If a client asks many questions, do you take it personally, or do you listen to understand? If a client is late in paying you, what mental movie do you play? In this context, consider the following responses:

1. **The FIGHT response**: Not a physical fight, but a mental determination of "We can do this. There is a solution. How can we move forward?"

2. **The FLIGHT response:** In conflict, this response would lead to avoidance, shutting down, enduring abuse, or abandoning a dream or vision.

3. **The FRIGHT response:** Fear triggers hesitation, indecisiveness, and worries about all the "what ifs."

Mental Fountains

Your business can become a fountain of hope, honor, and innovation. Think about how rhythm can support even healthy mental narratives. What are the possibilities for your business to influence your community positively? Consider the potential within your company and industry, attracting favor and excellence. Visualize what's possible when being a fountain as opposed to a drain. Just as the ocean draws many to its edge, envision your business rhythm attracting those who recognize the sound it emits.

"If you look the right way, you can see the whole world is a garden."
~ Hodgson Burnett

Opportunity Presents Itself - Nineteen Days

What's possible in nineteen days? Is your current business ready for the next opportunity? What would an opportunity look like for your business? What if the opportunity was within your area of expertise but had an expedited timeline? One day, I was presented with the challenge of building a story-and-a-half home in nineteen days. At first, I listened and understood the reason behind the nineteen-day timeframe. This understanding began to fuel us, getting our metaphorical rocket off the launch pad.

"The purpose of life is to live it, to taste experience to the utmost, to reach out eagerly and without fear for newer and richer experience."
~ Eleanor Roosevelt

Tangible and Intangible Rhythm

I requested one day to orchestrate the schedule and gather the entire team of vendors, subcontractors, and teammates—this was before reality television. At first, the initial response was, "What? You're kidding me, right?" Everyone's reaction was similar until they saw my conviction. They believed that we could finish this home in nineteen days.

Feeding and Fueling The Why

The "why" was what started to fuel us, but something very synergistic began to happen! It was like a domino effect. Everyone began to connect their ideas, teams, and resources and rally behind a bigger purpose as the homeowners stood in the distance overjoyed. The momentum built exponentially after day one. Literally, multiple things were taking place, like the rhythm of many instruments playing in an orchestra.

Working in two major twelve-hour shifts for almost nineteen days, the house was completed with a certificate of occupancy. What can we learn to apply to the vast possibilities of opportunities that knock on our doors? There was immense fulfillment for everyone who participated in building this home. This experience fostered a culture and respect for future unique projects. We all celebrated the teamwork, camaraderie, and interconnected synergy!

Context of New Growth

1. What is our business's initial response when a unique opportunity presents itself?
2. How could you build within your business culture an inspiring overcoming mindset?
3. A discovery that it takes a leader to carry the unwavering culture and context for the entire duration of the project.
4. What could you solve in your industry, creating large growth for your business?
5. During your huddles, how could you build into their beliefs that we always have solutions?

"You must live in the present, launch yourself on every wave, find your eternity in each moment. Fools stand on their island of opportunities and look toward another land. There is no other land; there is no other life but this." ~ Henry David Thoreau

I have been in the construction industry for over 25 years. Despite all the innovation, ideas, and technologies that have developed, changes are often met with resistance. We frequently hear, "This is the way we've always done it!" or "Here we go again!" These sentiments can sometimes be accompanied by harsh negative comments or a general negative disposition. However, what if we embraced this feedback as an opportunity for positive business growth? Consider taking a step back in your business and asking: Are there any mindsets within our culture that resist change because "this is the way we've always done it"?

Action Without Purpose

You may have heard the story about a young mom who always cut the end off the holiday ham. Her son asked, "Mom, why do you cut the end off the ham?"

She responded, "My mom always did it that way."

Intrigued, she picked up the phone and called her mom to ask, "Mom, why do you cut the end off the ham?"

Her mother thought for a moment and replied, "I think it might affect the taste. But let me call your grandma to be sure."

After calling, she got back to her daughter and said, with her daughter having put the call on speaker so her son could hear, "You won't believe it, but grandma cuts the end off because her pan was too small!"

They all laughed.

> *"The person who sets the frame of reference will be the one with the most influence." ~ Anthony Robbins*

Creative Awareness

1. Where in your business could you still be cutting the end of the ham?
2. Are there mindsets that entered the culture that could pivot back into rhythm?
3. What new supporting habits can help carry healthy rhythm?

"Determine that the thing....shall be done, and then [you] shall find the way." ~ Abraham Lincoln

Getting Unstuck & Staying Unstuck

Possibly, you're feeling stuck because you desire new growth but aren't sure how to achieve it. Maybe you're experiencing growth in one area of your business but feel stagnant in another. Being an entrepreneur or a manager leading others can sometimes be a lonely journey. Loneliness can creep in, often without us recognizing its onset or its warning signs. Fear and uncertainty can further contribute to this feeling of being stuck.

Awareness Questions:

1. What does being stuck look like?
2. What are the signs of being stuck?
3. How do you get unstuck?
4. How can you refuel your rhythm?

"Awareness precedes change." ~ Robin Sharma

Key One: Awareness

Awareness is a continuous skill vital for recognizing our own mental, emotional, and physical states. Thriving as a leader often hinges on this principle of awareness. Webster's Dictionary defines awareness as "knowledge and understanding that something is happening or exists." The first step to consider is exploring what the warning signs of being stuck might be. Having worked with numerous leaders over the past few decades, I've observed similar warning signs that are beneficial to recognize. Burying one's head in the sand or avoiding a situation rarely resolves the feeling of being stuck. Let's delve into some of these signs.

Warning Signs

1. Withdrawing from others, your team and peers.
2. No longer reading, listening to podcasts; personal development is nonexistent.
3. Avoiding feedback, coaching, and personal growth.
4. Resistance to your goals, dreams, vision, purpose, gifts, and talents.
5. Stopped dreaming and started despising the very reason you started. Dread settles in.
6. Become negative, critical, pessimistic. Complaining and consumed with comparing.
7. Inaction and indecisiveness; getting buried in clutter.
8. Breaking small commitments and avoiding growth activities.
9. Increased anxiety, depression, suspicion, and passivity.
10. It's difficult to be spontaneous and explore possibilities.

Key Two: Decrease the Unknowns

Think of when the Wright brothers invented the airplane. At first, people were not lining up to board the planes. With consistency, commitment, innovation, and overcoming gravity with the law of lift and thrust, flying today is a way of life for many. Technology and training have taken lots of UNKNOWNS out of the flying experience. The elimination of unknowns in the aviation industry is backed by brilliant people, technology, training, basic checklists for every flight, systems, team support, and a flight plan tailored to a specific destination. When a plane encounters turbulence, adjustments are made, but **the focus remains on the big picture**: reaching the destination safely.

Key Three: Power of Environment

Have you ever heard "walk on the sunny side of the street"? Your environment is like a greenhouse for growth. Clutter and chaos or order and peace? This is a simple but profound snapshot of the environment. How about the background noise of gossip or encouragement? What about the overall team culture? Is it filled with celebration and honor or negativity and dishonor? You're one choice away from building a new greenhouse that reproduces thriving growth. Begin with cleaning up clutter and with positive quotes, fresh decor, spring cleaning, and positive music. My intention is to create awareness of the power of the right environment to help you get unstuck!

"Starbucks was founded around the experience and the environment of their stores. Starbucks was about a space with comfortable chairs, lots of power outlets, tables and desks at which we could work and the option to spend as much time in their stores as we wanted without any pressure to buy. The coffee was incidental." ~ Simon Sinek

Key Four: Power of Connection

One way to take significant steps forward and break free from feeling stuck is by intentionally connecting with others. The giant sequoia trees stand tall and thrive through storms because their roots are interconnected. Just as a LEGO® piece stays engaged and fulfills its purpose when surrounded by other LEGO®s, a brick in a house is designed to be part of a masterpiece. It works together with other bricks to build a wall that withstands storms, protects the building it surrounds, and showcases beautiful architecture. Foster connections with people who support you, celebrate you, remain loyal, and bring out the best in you. The people that surround you can either be an elevator taking you up to the suite or a drain sucking the life from you!

"Invisible threads are the strongest ties."
~ Friedrich Nietzsche

"The most important things in life are the connections
you make with others." – Tom Ford

Key Five: Intentional Action

We briefly discussed some warning signs of being stuck. Now, let me highlight a few intentional action steps to move out of that state and stay unstuck. We're aware that a ship sailing the high seas doesn't provide a conducive environment for barnacles and algae to cling to its hull. Let's delve into some strategies to get unstuck.

Key Six: Feeding Momentum Staying Unstuck

1. Knowing you're part of a bigger purpose. Knowing your goal behind the goals!

2. Feed and grow your identity with life-giving attributes.

3. Look daily with your eyes at your dream board, goals, and declarations.

4. Our words form worlds; begin speaking life-giving, positive language.

5. Hire a qualified coach.

6. Surround yourself with a team. Avoid being a lone ranger.

7. You may or may not have heard of this simple, yet powerful, technique called the **"S.M.A.R.T. Technique."** A goal is not a wish or a dream; think of goals as steps on a staircase. For a goal to be effective, it must have a definitive, specific date and use relevant, positive, present-tense language. Well-written goals are short, positive, measurable, and intentional.

- **Specific**: Wording that specifies the goal.
- **Measurable**: Word the goal that it can be measured.
- **Attainable**: Is the goal a stretch but able to be accomplished?
- **Realistic/Risky**: The goal is not a wish; you're actually able to achieve it. A goal is a step toward greater vision.
- **Time/Date:** The time factor actually creates a commitment.

8. Establish healthy habits to carry your goals. Ask someone for accountability.

9. Declutter your personal and business space.

10. Walk on the sunny side of the road. Daily fresh air.

Key Seven: What's Possible Through Delegation

Consider delegating tasks to empower others to align with your vision and purpose. Often, as entrepreneurs, leaders, specialists, and managers, the mindset might lean towards handling everything ourselves. But give this a try: empower others by entrusting them with responsibilities. Think of it as "training for reigning." A baseball team has nine players because no single player can win the game alone. They train, get coached, and play practice games. To break free from stagnation and maintain momentum, engage your team to support you, allowing you to operate at your best. One of the greatest benefits to your team is when you excel in what you were born to do.

"We accomplish all that we do through delegation - either to time or to other people." ~ Stephen Covey

Awareness Questions for Discovery:

1. Why did you start your business, organization or take on that leadership role?
2. What is that core why, the goal behind the goal that fuels you daily? Write that down!
3. What is one step of action you can take today to get unstuck? Apply some of the list in "Feeding The Momentum Section."
4. What one self-sabotaging mindset pops up when you see adversity?
5. What could you do to flip the switch, feeding the positive promise of the negative mindset?

Key Eight: Recalibrate

Recalibration is a healthy process and is vital for leaders to stay unstuck. Think of your vehicle when you get a new set of tires: the mechanic balances the tires and then aligns them for maximum traction and wear and tear. Then they request after so many miles that you bring the vehicle in to rotate the tires. This is a form of recalibration to gain the maximum miles and safety.

Another example is P.D.C.A.— PLAN, DO, CHECK, ADJUST. Do a plan for a set time, then check the plan for results. Then, adjust, get feedback, and pivot. Finally, recalibrate with a new plan, repeating this process. Be willing to make changes.

Recalibration: "a change in the way you do or think about something."
~ Cambridge Dictionary

Key Nine: Rest

Rest is a powerful part of recalibration. Think of working out, which is beneficial, but overdoing it can cause damage. Set up rest stops, much like you would when traveling on long trips. We pull in, rest, recharge, recalibrate, eat, walk, and plan. Remember, each leader has a different capacity; recognize yours without comparing it to others. Rest is not idleness; it's intentional, habitual, enjoyable, healthy, and fun. Rest fuels your creativity to solve challenges. Consider exploring a hobby or activity that allows you to reset weekly.

"We must always change, renew and rejuvenate ourselves or
otherwise, we harden." ~ Johann Wolfgang Von Goethe

Final Thoughts

If you are stuck, I want to encourage you by reminding you that you have hope and a future. You're not a failure just because you feel stuck or are experiencing being stuck. Please take action today, reach forward, and take one step of action today. Remember, there is always a solution. You were born with a gift, with talent, and you're worthy of connection. I also encourage you to go back and reread the blogs on our website.

"We cannot solve our problems with the same thinking we used
when we created them." ~ Albert Einstein

Overcome Frustration: The Lens of Gratitude

Are you experiencing frustration with your business, team, or situation? Does the thought of quitting, retreating, or the lack of focus blur your vision or purpose? Allow me to reframe frustration through the lens of gratitude! Perhaps you're experiencing frequent thoughts of discouragement and uncertainty, and you're longing for more in life and business. What if we explore a step to transform the meaning of frustration and flip the switch on those thoughts to catapult you, your team, and your business to greater success? What if your frustration is a knock of opportunity, setting you up for promotion and prominence?

"Show me someone who has done something worthwhile, and I'll show you someone who has overcome adversity." ~ Lou Holtz

CHAPTER NINE

Your Perspective Lens

New Lens of Perspective

Let's take a moment to reframe frustration and see through a growth catalyst lens! Let's flip the switch, so to speak! What happens when someone sits on the other end of a seesaw? Their body weight launches you higher! Frustration may feel like a weight or a wall, but what if it's possible that you're simply being set up for great growth, connections, and innovation?

Think of your eye doctor who flips different lenses over your eyes, asking, "Number one or number two?" The doctor's goal is to provide corrective lenses to eliminate blurred vision and restore clear sight. Blurred vision is frustrating, but not acknowledging it could mean missing out on the gift of clear vision. What if we applied a new "gratitude" lens to frustration? With this new perspective, it's possible that our views, thoughts, reactions, and discussions about events, situations, or relationships might change for the better.

"Fire is the test of gold; adversity, of strong men."
~ Martha Graham

Growth Through Gratitude

What is gratitude? Gratitude is an expression, a value, or an appreciation for what a person has. Consider how to take a next step, applying the lens of gratitude, feeding, and fueling Synergistic Rhythm.

Gratitude is a transformed inner heart, a renewed mind perspective manifesting itself through our attitudes, character, and choices. We all have heard the saying, an attitude of gratitude. Remember the picture of the eye doctor putting on corrective lenses for clear vision? Clear vision creates clarity, certainty, and a confidence of direction! Clear vision allows us to see opportunities through the eyes of promise! What if we drop the lens of gratitude – a transformed perspective – over frustration or adversity? A constant state, lens, or mindset of frustration or discontentment can foster unhealthy choices, redirecting the vision. Let's harness this opportunity and explore possibilities and potential, flipping the meaning of frustration.

> *"As with the butterfly, adversity is necessary to build character in people." ~ Joseph B. Wirthlin*

Gratitude is a Lens Cleaner

Those of us who wear glasses, sunglasses, or contacts all use some form of lens cleaner. Without regular cleaning, the accumulated dirt and smudges can amplify frustration and influence our attitudes. Take a moment to consider: where is most of your current frustration stemming from? I once heard that a combat pilot is constantly making adjustments to stay on course.

To aid in cleansing and re-establishing a thriving perspective, what if we deliberately applied the lens of gratitude to our hearing, to what we read, and even when confronted with criticism, doubt, or fear? What if we adjusted our perception of all we absorb, filtering out the negativity, and chose to see through a lens of gratitude instead? Directing and bolstering your vision and purpose can be likened to molding clay with your hands, fostering growth, confidence, and cohesion, all while building an inspiring leadership culture!

"You'll never find a better sparring partner than adversity."
~ Golda Meir

Art and Science of Leadership

In leadership, there is both an art side and a science side. Think of the art side as the **heart side**. It's like a pianist playing with their heart instead of their head! We experience their personality and body inflections; their soul is felt through the piano! We all understand how important it is to put our hearts into something bigger than ourselves, flowing from the foundation within our souls. Gratitude activates a life-giving place in the heart where others experience a fountain of music! Gratitude is a very healthy form of rhythm. The science side of leadership is the important and technical how-to side of leadership. It's more of the mechanical or knowledge side of leadership. Healthy leadership is combining the science side with the **(ART) HEART SIDE.**

Steps of Action: Applying Gratitude - Gratitude Feeds Thriving Rhythm

1. For the next seven days, counter negative thoughts by replacing them with thoughts of gratitude!
2. Consider what questions you could ask your team to foster a culture of gratitude.

3. Ask your team for one WIN for the day or week. This switches the focus to a positive, celebration culture!

4. Feed and fuel gratitude by asking curiosity questions. What feeds and fuels your team?

5. Consider writing daily WINS, repositioning focus on gratitude! You can look back at this like a rainy day note!

How We See Creates New Opportunity

There is a term in leadership: **"FACT MEANING."** The way we perceive an event and the significance we attach to a situation, event, or even a frustration can affect our capacity for creative solutions. The fact is, stuff happens; the significance we assign to it can either hinder us or ignite our passion. For instance, if someone says "no" during your sales call, it doesn't necessarily mean you're not a good salesperson. The interpretation a person gives to that "no" can be a game changer.

Applying the lens of gratitude for your colleagues, teammates, and customers can greatly change our view of all relationships! What is possible if our systems and business culture overflow with gratitude? Think of how you feel when someone is grateful for you. Think of how you feel when someone expresses an act of kindness. Gratitude works like a magnet, attracting opportunity to the business. Consistently feeding a culture of gratitude will uplift attitudes and increase team efficiency!

"A challenge only becomes an obstacle when you bow to it." ~ Ray Davis

What are the Possibilities with Frustrations?

For example, perhaps your current frustration is creating internal tension. Even in the most difficult times, consider looking at the test as training! Ask questions about the frustration. How can I/we create through this frustration? What choice could be made to flip the switch? What new meaning can be attached during the frustration? For example, attach a new meaning to a "no" during sales. The temptation is to take a "no" personally when it's an opportunity to pivot, grow, and adjust your approach. The frustration is like a dashboard light giving you feedback! The meaning a salesperson or a business leader attaches to a "no" can be a game changer!

The Seed from Adversity

Adversity holds the "seed" potential to unlock creativity, innovation, and growth. Your core values will act like a GPS, defining and reminding you of your purpose, focus, and what to say "yes" to. View adversity as an opportunity to validate, affirm, and develop greater effectiveness and efficiency!

Healthy core values applied during times of frustration and adversity can be like a pacesetter on a track leaping hurdles! Here is a perspective to consider: the current frustration is preparing you for a breakthrough, renaissance, a rebirth, a setup, a new launch!

"Start by doing what's necessary; then do what's possible; and suddenly you're doing the impossible." ~ Francis of Assisi

Resistance Builds Muscle

Think for a moment of when you desire to tone up and do so by doing push-ups, sit-ups, stretching, and you start to experience resistance. The goal may be wellness, more energy, and a healthier demeanor. It's in the consistent resistance over time that your body responds by getting stronger and more defined! What if the resistance that you're experiencing with an event, situation, or relationship could fuel personal and business development? What if, through applying the lens of gratitude, the resistance fuels greater team building, tenacity, and fortitude, creating greater customer and team retention?

"Life keeps throwing me stones. And I keep finding the diamonds."
~ Ana Claudia Antunes

New Habit: Celebrating Wins

One way to keep a team, business, family, or yourself energized is continuously celebrating the wins, the victories, and the milestones! Celebrating the forward growth, the small accomplishments, and hitting goals fuels the inspiration! Another habit to consider is cultivating a culture of honor by cultivating transparency on a team through personal growth discoveries! This can start with the leader and filter into the organization. These transparent discoveries are from a place of overcoming victory, not a context of dumping. Being vulnerable does not mean a toxic daily dump!

Notice that cultivating a culture of honor with intention fuels positive attitudes, mindsets, and awareness for growth! This starts to feed your business rhythm in your ecosystem, which creates authentic connection on a team! Celebrating one another's overcoming victories keeps a team closer and creates an enjoyable work environment. Have a blast flipping the meaning of frustration and launching a new growth season!

"No person was ever honored for what he received. Honor has been the reward for what he gave." ~ Calvin Coolidge

Power of Passion

Passion is like fuel to the fire and feeds rhythm! It will feed your vision, energizing your business rhythm! Passion is why we do what we do!

Passion is like the catalyst that makes sparkling water bubble. Passion is the light that speaks louder than words. We all know when it's present. We understand teams that have it. We can see the flicker in the eyes of a client when they are passionate about your goods or services. Passion is a powerful, strong emotion. We put wood on a fire to fuel it. Fire needs oxygen to burn well. Passion is like oxygen!

Power of Vision

Vision is what it looks like when it's built. A designer may ask, what is your vision for your new home? When the home is built, it looks like the design, which was rooted in the vision. Vision is what we see! Goals are like steps to a vision. Think of goals like a staircase to the next floor. Every company needs a vision that is active and thriving. When a business is thriving, it looks like something. It's what it looks like when it's built. That is not by accident. Is your business going in the direction of your vision?

Passion Fuels Vision

Think of passion like gasoline; it fuels the vehicle. Without gas, the vehicle is not going far. Passion is the rocket fuel that thrusts the vision. What in your business makes you come alive? If the visionary is passionate about the vision and business, it will fuel others on the team.

Vision Steers Passion

Now, with both vision and passion, they work synergistically together. The vision is the destination, and it's like the rocket being blasted off the pad. Without the vision acting as a rudder on a ship, so to speak, passion will be like fireworks shooting off, sending them off dangerously and aimlessly without focus. Passion, without vision alignment, will foster discouragement because there are no tangible results. What steps could you and your team take to fuel the vision with passion? How can you steer the vision that's driven by passion to see steps taken, creating noticeable results?

POWER OF PASSION FUELING VISION AND VISION STEERING PASSION.

Business Pain Point Questions

To create awareness of recurring pain points, let's assess potential growth opportunities to solve:

1. What keeps you from hitting your growth targets?
2. How is the quality of your leads?
3. How do you navigate the tension between current customers and attracting qualified new customers?
4. How would you describe your ability to navigate priority and boundaries with your schedule?
5. What are you avoiding that can be solved?
6. What one thing, if you stop doing it, would allow greater growth?
7. What process is in place to grow, inspire, and inform your teams?
8. What keeps you up at night?
9. What aspects of your role don't you like?
10. Where could you shift your time to allow greater growth?
11. What are the key solutions you desire in your business?
12. What role brings you the greatest joy personally?
13. How would you evaluate your ability to navigate conflict?
14. If you were to give yourself feedback, what would you say?
15. What do you dread with your business?

CHAPTER TEN

Shaking Can Reveal The Gold

Golden Opportunity

I visited an old gold mine in Colorado and was intrigued by the history of gold mining. For fun, they offered an opportunity to pan for gold. Four pans were available, so I thought, *Let's go for it!* It seemed a bit silly as the facilitator kept saying, "Shake, shake, shake." This simple process involved sifting through the fine dirt to see if any gold was present.

Shaking Reveals The Gold

The first person quit almost immediately, and the second gave up a minute later. It definitely required patience. I asked, "May I have their pans?"

The facilitator agreed, and then the third person offered, "Here, you can have mine too!"

I continued to "shake, shake, shake." Gold was revealed in each pan, one at a time. I smiled, thinking, *Wow, what a great life lesson!* I wonder how many people give up on their vision, their business, or their goals just before the gold is revealed.

Knowing There's Gold

I thought, *Wow, this is just like confronting a superficial belief or fear of failure.* All three people thought it was too silly. What if, with a relentless commitment to steering your business rhythm, the gold within your vision is showcased in a thriving manner? There is gold within your business.

Gold in Serving Others:

I asked the facilitator how they separate the small pieces of gold in their mining process. He smiled and shared a story with me. He said many years ago, one of the miner's wives was looking for ways to earn extra money, so she asked her husband to see if she could wash any of his fellow workers' clothes. So he brought home a few overalls, and during the washing, she discovered something amazing.

From Soap Bubbles To Gold

She saw all these tiny dust particles of gold floating on the top of the water. She realized the soap was bringing the light gold dust to the surface. So she very carefully skimmed the water, placing the gold dust in a can. She asked her husband if she could wash the clothes of all his fellow workers. Over time, she filled that can with gold, pioneering a process that utilized water and a certain soap to separate gold. Through this, I also learned that serving others created golden opportunities and innovative solutions. How many "golden" opportunities might be hidden in mundane tasks, like doing someone's laundry, so to speak? My experience that day was incredibly empowering! What would it be like to stay the course in your business, shaking away the excess dirt to reveal the gold beneath? Even if you've quit in the past, pick up a pan and start sifting, shaking away the excess chatter, clutter, and chaos. This method of mining for gold has its own rhythm.

Meaning Attached to Events

In business, when you're focused on developing sales and growing teams, unexpected events or situations can arise either from external factors beyond our control or due to specific business choices. For instance, in sales, a potential client might decline an offer. Alternatively, they might pose numerous questions about the value of your products, pricing, quality, or service. However, this doesn't necessarily reflect negatively on the value of your products or services. Sometimes, during growth phases in business, you might encounter resistance from team members, face economic challenges, or grapple with the overall capacity to manage this growth. Let me share a catalyst opportunity to scale your business: you can flip the meaning associated with such events. This approach can positively influence your business rhythm.

"Leadership is about taking responsibility, not making excuses."
~ Anonymous

The Value From an Event

Many leaders view events and resistance as negative outcomes. But what if these events represent opportunities for significant growth? For instance, if during a sales pitch you consistently hear responses like "no" or "not interested," and you always perceive this feedback as negative, it could potentially steer your business's growth in a downward trajectory. But what happens when there's a hiccup in cash flow or a glitch in production? What if, instead of panicking, we flip the switch, illuminating the room of opportunity, and begin to explore creative solutions to turn these events into value-adding experiences for the business? What if the overarching mindset was to use such events as catalysts for growth? For instance, mastering sales objections or pivoting resources, reallocating hours, enhancing development, and even customer service could all add greater value to the enterprise.

"We must look at the lens through which we see the world, as well as the world we see, and that the lens itself shapes how we interpret the world."
~Stephen R. Covey

Feedback Is Gold

What if it's possible to foster a rhythm in your business culture where feedback is considered gold? Think of it as "breakfast for champions." What if, during the hiring process, there's a business culture training that emphasizes a positive, solution-oriented mindset, rather than a pessimistic or negative one? Challenges are inevitable. However, it's the response to those challenges that can make all the difference. Imagine creating a business culture that welcomes feedback, not as a judgment of a person's motives, but simply as a means to foster dynamic growth. Such feedback can enhance the synergistic component, with synergy meaning many parts working together simultaneously. How can you use feedback to strengthen your business rhythm?

"There is no failure. Only feedback."
~ Robert Allen

Our View of an Event

I remember working on a high-end home, renovating the basement. We took protective measures at the first-floor entry leading to the basement. The tape we used claimed it could be left down for seven days. However, when we removed it on the fifth day, the finish came off with the tape. At first, my heart raced in panic. But we immediately focused on finding a solution and devised a win-win plan.

When we brought this to the homeowners' attention, they were blown away by our candor and then impressed by the solutions we proposed to create a significant win for them. We refinished their entire first floor. Based on how we addressed and handled this situation, they hired us for another large project. We had followed the tape's instructions precisely but still encountered a problem. Sometimes, even when you do everything correctly, there are still opportunities to rise to the occasion and go for the gold.

"If you believe it will work out, you'll see opportunities. If you believe it won't, you will see obstacles." ~ Wayne Dyer

The Right Mental Movie

Many events will inevitably happen, but the significance a business or team attaches to them can be the game changer. What if feedback became an integral part of your daily and weekly huddles? Consider the potential of adjusting the team's mindset, ensuring they maintain the right mental imagery. Think about a gold medalist. Despite factors like weather, the opposing team's size and skill, or their personal feelings, they have to maintain the right mental attitude. When the game clock starts, it's essential to give it their all and play their best because this isn't a dress rehearsal.

"Nothing can stop the man with the right mental attitude from achieving his goal: nothing on earth can help the man with the wrong mental attitude." ~ Unknown

No Excuses Mindset

Think of it this way: What if the business culture refrained from making excuses and instead asked, "How can I serve you?" In other words, make significant commitments and produce significant results. Napoleon Hill once said, "Every adversity, every failure, every heartache carries with it the seed of an equal or greater benefit." What about placing such importance on the opportunity to refine, reimagine, or reinvent your systems, people, or culture? The ability of a business to reinterpret events and situations can present a tremendous innovative opportunity.

"A 'No Excuses' mindset does recognize the reality of your situation, but its emphasis is not on how to validate the condition. Instead, it should be on how to solve the challenge the situation describes." ~ Farshad Asl

The Rhythm Opportunity

1. Which event can your business reinterpret to create a growth opportunity?
2. During your team huddles, what creative ways can you implement an idea exchange to explore the meaning of events as feedback?
3. What action steps can you take to serve your customers, flipping the switch from a potential negative to a positive?

When An Idea Touches The Heart

What is possible when an idea touches the heart of a leader? What's possible with the influence of that idea within your team and business? The potential from that ripple effect inspires and impacts every area of your life and business. I heard a quote by Victor Hugo: "No force on earth can stop an idea whose time has come!"

"Ideas are the beginning points of all fortunes."
~ Napoleon Hill

Breathe Into The Idea

Think of when a stone is cast into a pond; there is a ripple effect touching the edge! I remember, as a young child, throwing stones into ponds and waiting and watching with anticipation for the ripple to touch the entire pond's edge! This idea of touching the heart, the mind, and emotion fed with purposeful passion can feed your business rhythm in a fresh new way. Breathing inspiration into the idea can open doors! What idea could you discover to solve the biggest challenges? Remember, businesses get paid to solve challenges. Challenges viewed properly are great opportunities to serve and create abundant win-win.

"A mediocre idea that generates enthusiasm will go further than a great idea that inspires no one." ~ Mary Kay Ash

An Idea is Like A Seed

What if the idea feeds hope so big within you that it ignites a passion deep in your core? That idea awakening something deep within you rising up deep within you? Think of this idea as wind filling a sail, moving the sailboat forward. What would be possible if that sail of the idea was fed, empowered, and explored? Consider the nature of a seed; it will reproduce after its kind. For a seed to grow, it has to be planted in the hearts of others. Let's explore some ideas to plant this concept so it can flourish.

"Ideas can be life-changing. Sometimes all you need to open the door is just one more good idea." ~ Jim Rohn

The Process of Becoming

I encourage that that past event or situation is not who you are! What if this idea is the bow for the arrow? The past tension is utilized as a motivator to feed the idea whose time has come. You may be tired or not sure if you want to risk it again. Hope deferred can be like setting the table and pulling the tablecloth out, and all the dishes and work have to be done all over again! Ask, what are you becoming in the process? What are you building? The Wright brothers had an idea whose time had come. They also had a few opportunities to get off the ground successfully.

Feed The Seed

If the idea is like a seed, and the heart of the business is like the soil, what if we feed the seed potential of that idea? Let's explore a few practical ways to implement an idea exchange.

> *"The ability to convert ideas to things is the secret of outward success."*
> *~ Henry Ward Beecher*

Idea Exchange Process:

1. You personally write and journal on the idea before telling one person.
2. Feeding this idea within you with research and inspiration.
3. Then, share with one very trusted, big-thinking associate.
4. Gather 3-5 core leaders sharing your passionate idea without refining it.
5. Note: The temptation is to jump right into refining, which is a trap and can get into the weeds. Weeds kill garden life.
6. Then, as the leader, take what you heard from your trusted colleagues and build a list of power questions to water the heart garden.
7. Initiate another meeting with the same 3-5 and ask questions and list answers on a whiteboard. Circle the key actionable next steps.

8. Ask, how can this idea fuel and feed our Synergistic Rhythm? How can this idea add value to our clients and systems, people, and culture? What are the costs of not exploring the idea? What is the seed potential of this idea?

9. Creating buy-in first before sharing the idea. Others will fuel you and develop other vision carriers with this idea. Remember, there are critics and dream stealers. At the same time, it's all only feedback and not personal.

10. The final part is implementing an idea. Think effective planning, communication of the value, creating buy-in with the closest leaders. Consider doing everything possible with excellence. Remember earlier, we talked about—Plan, Do, Check and Adjust.

Nourish and Weed The Idea

Remember, gardens require nourishment and weeding. Steve Jobs innovated the computer with new ideas. He pioneered Apple! UPS brought their team together, saving the company millions through an idea exchange by only making right turns when possible. When one idea is put into motion, it has the power to touch the entire business and customers, even the marketplace! A fresh new idea has a way to be a catalyst boosting enthusiasm, retention, and attracting new business development!

"If you have an apple and I have an apple, and we exchange these apples, then you and I will still each have one apple. But if you have an idea and I have an idea, and we exchange these ideas, then each of us will have two ideas." ~ George Bernard Shaw

Customer Service Has A Rhythm

What is possible when your whole team captures the essence of world-class customer service? Long-lasting customer service flows from a heart connection with your clients or customers. Many companies might offer the same product or service, but the relational connection you have cannot be marketed. Customers will drive the extra miles to feel understood, to feel valued, and to feel like they're not just another transaction. Consider asking, "Are we relational or transactional in our customer service?" Then, think about how to develop the genuine heart behind customer service.

"Make the customer the hero of your story."
~ Ann Handley

Going The Extra Mile

I remember going to a local steak shop that was always filled with lots of laughter and a relational connection with the owner. He was always out among the people connecting, playing games with those seated. He was lighthearted. He always brought fruit and vegetables from the local growers into his restaurant and gave them away for free. His pickup truck was full. His steak shop was full because people felt his heart!

"There are no traffic jams on the extra mile."
~ Roger Staubach, NFL Hall of Famer

Personal Responsibility

Customer service from the heart is a choice that each person makes to go the extra mile in serving. What could you do that would stand out in your customer service that's authentic and from the heart? How could you add so much value to the customer care and experience that people feel and connect with the culture of your business and colleagues?

> *"The goal as a company is to have customer service that is not just the best, but legendary." ~ Sam Walton*

Building Rhythm Through Trust

Recently, I watched rock climbers scaling a 150-foot-high rock wall. Watching them work as a team, I saw that they communicated constantly, guiding each other through the best path and maximizing their ropes and safety clips. They had created a very high level of trust with each other, their navigation abilities, and their equipment. They made it look like anyone could climb a high rock wall. When trust is present, it avoids injuries, creates safety, and it allows new possibilities to be accomplished.

> *"Nothing is as fast as the speed of trust. Nothing better accelerates a transaction, a task, or project, than trust. When there is a high level of trust between parties in a business transaction, deals can be made in minutes with a handshake, yet many organizations are dysfunctional and inefficient because of low-trust cultures." ~ Stephen Covey*

> *"Trust is the 'hidden variable' in the formula for organizational success. The old paradigm was that Strategy x Execution = Results. The new paradigm is that Strategy x Execution x Trust = Results. Trust always affects two outcomes: speed and cost." ~ Stephen Covey*

What is possible in cultivating a culture of trust? Consistency within your systems, people, and culture in alignment with core values will create a greenhouse for trust to grow and thrive. Here are simple but effective people skills to scale higher heights.

Few Actions to Practice Daily - Fostering Trust

1. Keep simple commitments
2. Initiate acts of kindness
3. Listen to Understand
4. Acknowledge someone doing something well
5. Honor your teammates and boss/managers
6. Ask others open-ended questions
7. Invite feedback from your team
8. Handle conflict as soon as possible

High Impact - Low-Risk Questions

To foster thriving growth, mastering powerful questions is crucial. It's a skill that can be learned and emanate authentically from genuine curiosity to understand or show interest. Powerful questions require more than a simple "yes" or "no" answer. If you desire better results with your people and customers, consider this approach: Ask high-impact, low-risk questions. When possible, avoid making statements that might foster judgment or elicit negative reactions.

"Listening is a magnetic and strange thing, a creative force. The friends who listen to us are the ones we move toward. When we are listened to, it creates us, makes us unfold and expand." ~ Karl A. Menniger

Powerful Questions

What is a powerful question? Learning the art and science of asking questions is another key to developing and sustaining Synergistic Rhythm. Powerful questions will be key to continuing to grow your systems, people, culture, and core values. A powerful question cares enough about the person that your question engages them to open up about a topic. For example, what are a couple of things you enjoy about your favorite restaurant? Powerful questions are asked from a context of authentic curiosity. They never make a person feel like they're in trouble, judged, or on a witness stand, so to speak. Powerful questions foster dynamic openness and explore greater depths in any area of business. They build a relational connection rather than a transactional one. Powerful questions allow the other person to express themselves and share their thoughts.

"One of the most sincere forms of respect is actually listening to what another has to say." ~ Bryant H. McGill

Examples of Powerful Questions

1. What are three goals you have in the next six months?
2. How would you describe your business's greatest strength?
3. What is one major adversity you overcame in your business?
4. How did you apply what you learned from that adversity?
5. How does your greatest passion in business fuel you to keep going?

Non-Impact Questions

Non-impact questions require only a "yes" or "no" answer. These types of questions create no real engagement. For example: "Do you like blue?" The engagement can be over in a moment. "Do you like our price?" They can answer "yes" or "no." Developing the soft skill of authentic relational engagement cultivates a deeper connection with all people. In sales and business, it allows you to serve and honor with a greater measure of effectiveness.

"You cannot truly listen to anyone and do anything else at the same time." ~ M. Scott Peck

Examples of Low-Impact Questions

1. Do you like this color?
2. Making statements are high risk: Your attitude is off today! Can't you do anything right today?
3. Avoid using word statements like, you always, you never, you need to, why don't you listen?
4. When are you going to change?
5. Can you dress a little differently?

Notice how the context of these questions is high risk. This means you can lose clients and colleagues. People never want to feel judged or punished. In business, mastering the art and skill of dealing with people will allow you to flourish. One key principle is to give up your right to be right! Learn to adapt your questions to show authentic curiosity.

The Heart of The Conversation

When we engage in conversation, we listen not only to the words but also to the heart and context behind them. Additionally, we should pay attention to what isn't being shared. Is there hesitation or avoidance of certain topics? In sales, you might hear the customer's words, but they could actually imply something opposite to what they are saying. Listening with the intent to understand is crucial for determining the next powerful question to ask. For instance, if a potential client shifts away from the presented value and avoids making a commitment, it may simply indicate that they need to develop a greater sense of trust, security, and understanding of the value you're presenting. It's essential to remember that questions don't imply disinterest. Nor do they suggest that your product or service isn't valuable or high-quality simply because they're seeking more information. It's never personal. By quickly internalizing that it's not personal, you can build purposeful momentum to drive sales and growth.

> *"The most important thing in communication is hearing what isn't said"* ~ *Peter Drucker*

Avoid Questions With Assumptions

For example, there are questions that carry judgment with them. Direct questions filled with judgments can be very high-risk, low-impact, and potentially very costly. Examples include asking, "Why are you late again?" or asking a client, "Why haven't you returned my call?"

Rhythm Between Following and Leading

To become a dynamic, influential leader requires a heart that understands the profound influence of following well. In this context, "following well" is rooted in honoring those you are interconnected with. A leader of influence may or may not have a positional title. A thriving follower who serves with honor will ultimately be recognized by all with whom they are interconnected.

Recognizing The Whole Team

A business leader cultivating a culture of honor, continuing to steer into its Synergistic Rhythm, will view each follower as an integral part of the business. Over the years, in our business culture, there has been a mindset that views followers as being lesser than leaders. However, both are integral parts of Synergistic Rhythm.

Listen to Understand

Value all on the team by listening to understand. Ask powerful questions and hear their feedback.

CHAPTER ELEVEN

Feeding and Steering Momentum

The Power of Momentum

When you think of momentum, what is the first thing you think of? Maybe it's a train moving consistently toward its destination? The professional surfer that rides that wave to the shore? Possibly, it's when you're traveling on vacation, making great memories with low stress. Or if you love sports, when you see your favorite football team in the zone, play after play, moving the ball successfully down the field!

> *"Momentum is whatever your attitude determines it to be."*
> *~ Lou Holtz*

What fuels a team to play until the last second runs out? What drives a surfer to risk their life on a hundred-foot wave? Could it be their "why"— the goal behind the goal—that fuels the momentum? Webster defines momentum as "strength or force gained by motion or by a series of events." What does momentum look like in your business? When momentum is present within your team, what results do you see? Let's explore a few keys to nurture momentum, ignite your business momentum, and guide it."

"Keep moving ahead because action creates momentum, which in turn creates unanticipated opportunities." ~ *Nick Vujicic*

Starting Momentum

A question to start your business momentum is: "What are you building?" Like many of the concepts in this book that support cultivating a thriving Synergistic Rhythm, momentum is another essential component. Remember, it's challenging to steer a parked car or a ship anchored to a pier. What does it look like when your business is in full momentum? What do the vision, purpose, and mission look like when they're fully realized in your business? The aim is to nurture momentum in such a way that it drives your business rhythm, facilitating growth. Consider momentum like a surfer patiently waiting for the wave to build. Initiating momentum involves casting vision and clarifying the "why" behind that vision. A common pitfall is to become mired in information without inspiration. The goal is not just to convey the vision, but to do so inspiringly! It's the passion behind what you're building momentum for that matters. Think of inspiration as the fuel that ignites the flame, and consider it akin to sunlight nurturing growth in a garden.

"Build confidence and momentum with each good decision you make from here on out and choose to be inspired." ~ *Joe Rogan*

Action Steps to Consider

1. Write what you see after the vision is built.
2. Write what inspires you about the vision and purpose.
3. List the benefits of having momentum working for you.
4. At this stage, it's not as important about the "how-tos" but the deep-held belief that inspires the why.
5. What is the goal behind the goal?

Feeding Momentum

Think of the surfer. They wait patiently for the right wave, letting wave after wave roll by. What is actually happening? The wave is building from the energy out in the ocean, rolling into shore. The key to feeding momentum is patience to nurture different aspects of vision simultaneously.

"The rhythm of daily action aligned with your goals creates the momentum that separates dreamers from super-achievers." ~ Darren Hardy

Inspire Core Leaders - Feeds Momentum

To fuel your business momentum, consider starting with one or two core leaders to establish buy-in. First, define the core "why" and then articulate it in a manner that inspires these leaders. Momentum needs vision carriers and influencers. Collaborate with them to develop a strategy, ensuring there's clarity on both the primary goal and the underlying reasons for it. Engage your key leaders with a steadfast commitment to maintain this momentum. Seek their dedication to uphold the inspiration. Treat all questions they pose as feedback—an opportunity to understand what they perceive and interpret. Drawing a parallel to the large home where everyone convened, ask yourself how to embed a value that goes beyond the superficial.

"One way to keep momentum going is to have constantly greater goals." ~ Michael Korda

Action Items to Consider

1. Life-giving, inspiring communication.

2. Consistently communicating with clarity.
3. Avoid getting into the weeds with too many details.
4. Inspiration then information.
5. Build buy-in with core leaders first.

"Commitment is the ignitor of momentum." ~ Peg Wood

Steering Momentum

Continuing with our surfer example, after they are on the wave and it's carrying them, they steer their surfboard by shifting their body weight. When potholes appear on the highway, we steer around them but keep going. Steering your momentum is a subtle shift, pivot, or embracing feedback from a teammate or customer. Remember, you cannot steer a parked car or a ship tied to the pier. Simultaneously feeding your momentum in many creative ways while steering can be quite effective. Your vision serves as the target, your passion as the fuel, and inspired leaders as the builders and carriers of momentum. When traveling, we use a GPS to guide us to our destination. The GPS doesn't power the journey; instead, it provides feedback on time, road hazards, speed, and places to stop for food.

Action Items to Consider

1. Identify potential distractions, potholes, and obstacles to overcome.
2. What is your business GPS?
3. What is the team's passion level?
4. What can you do when your business GPS gives you feedback?
5. Who is steering the momentum?

Results From Momentum

Ultimately, the momentum produces a result. What is the goal behind the goal? For example, increasing sales by 20% may be a goal. The goal behind that may be to serve and provide a world-class customer experience. How would you and your leaders describe the end result from steadfast momentum? Learning from the past in your business, what were a few keys in operation during momentous seasons?

"When you have momentum in the business, everything seems to roll forward, stuff gets done, things happen, employees are proactive, customers are happy and extraordinary results are produced."
~ Benard Mokua

Leaders Lead With Rhythm

Consider a graceful swan gliding across the water; it stands out and draws you in. Ever wonder why? It's their nature, their rhythm, their way. A swan's graceful rhythm is attractive and often causes many to pause and reflect. John Maxwell said, "Leaders become great, not because of their power, but because of their ability to empower others." Leaders who empower others through their beingness and attitudes—even without words—can ignite and model rhythm. Leaders have an extraordinary opportunity to influence the business culture and the context they desire to see within their teams. In the simplest way, just as the swan on the water carries a culture that is influenced simply by its graceful ways, so can a leader.

"It is your passion that empowers you to be able to do that thing you were created to do." ~ T. D. Jakes

Rhythm as a Leader

In track and field, there is a concept known as a runner's stride. A runner decides to push beyond their physical resistance, drawing from the depths of their heart. For an elite runner, rhythm and stride become a mental decision. There's an adage that says, "Run with your heart instead of your legs." Great runners will often have a pacesetter run alongside them on the track, setting and pushing their pace.

Record Breaking Rhythm

I talked earlier about Roger Bannister, the first person to break the 4-minute mile in 1954. He made a mental decision: today is the day! A key factor was practicing with a couple of pacemakers: Chris Chataway and Chris Brasher. They set the pace for Bannister, providing him with a consistent rhythm necessary to shatter all the negative mindsets, claiming it was biologically impossible. His pacemakers were the catalyst in establishing the rhythm. He had to make a decisive shift in his mental game to overcome history and the known biological constraints.

> *"I am not a product of my circumstances. I am a product of my decisions." ~ Stephen Covey*

Questions to Consider

1. Who is your pacesetter?
2. What mental movie is played when facing resistance?
3. How would you describe your leadership rhythm?

Sharpening the Edge

Roger Bannister had to be consistently out on the track to develop endurance, stamina, willpower, and muscle power, as well as expand his lung capacity! He sharpened his edge with a consistent daily routine. He sharpened his edge with the influence of pacesetters and coaching. Through his determination and rhythm, Bannister's extraordinary example broke the mindset barrier for approximately 1,500 people to run the mile in less than 4 minutes. The resistance his body felt fueled him to stay sharp.

"Give me six hours to chop down a tree and I will spend the first four sharpening the axe." ~ Abraham Lincoln

Keeping The Edge

We all know how frustrating it is to use a dull knife in the kitchen. In principle, a dull knife is an unsafe knife. Keeping the edge sharp requires intentional effort. Football teams huddle to make mental shifts with plays and to give high-fives, emphasizing the power of mental preparation. If your mind is like a plot of land, what are you planting in it to encourage growth? Where I walk, there's a large field overrun with weeds. This beautiful, flat piece of land holds great potential, but without intentional seeding, weeds will take over.

Your mental mindsets and beliefs are crucial for a thriving business rhythm. We are beings of constant thought, and our thoughts influence our choices. Which mindset would it benefit you to nurture and grow over the next season to achieve your goals?

"If you only have a hammer, you tend to see every problem as a nail." ~ Abraham Maslow

Questions to Consider

1. What if you read 15 minutes daily of a life-giving book supporting the mindset of where you desire to go?
2. What two or three people do you desire to speak into your thinking?
3. How could you eliminate the negative voices feeding your thinking?

"Write it on your heart that every day is the best day in the year."
~ Ralph Waldo Emerson

The Super Power of Words

Consider the superheroes from our childhood; each possessed unique superpowers. Now, reflect on a moment when someone spoke transformative words into your life, destiny, or business. The strength carried by a single word or a concise phrase can alter the course of history. Recall the word or phrase that sparked a change in your life or business. What potential does our power of speech hold?

Recognizing a Gift

I can distinctly remember a facilitator, Janet Henze, who said to me, "Ed, you have a gift! You have a gift for holding context in facilitation. You're a facilitator, and I have my eyes on you!" Those words pierced my heart and belief systems. I understood their meaning. For years, she modeled transformative work, and deep down, I longed to do what she did. She was acknowledging my gift of facilitation. There was something incredibly powerful when she spoke those words while looking into my eyes. I realized that her influence in my life was profound! Her words carried tremendous weight and had a significant impact on me.

"Words can inspire. And words can destroy. Choose yours well."
~ Robin Sharma

Words Carry Rhythm and Destiny

At first, her words took me by surprise, but they also ignited something within me! I felt this incredible surge in my soul. Then, the barrage of "how-tos" swamped my thoughts. I received her timely, powerful words wholeheartedly, like a thirsty person in the desert! Over that week, her words took root in my heart, as if a high-voltage switch had been flipped, illuminating a city. Words have the power to activate and nourish life, or to delay, destruct, and destroy. With leadership comes the responsibility to use our words to foster a vibrant culture. Our words have the power to create, to activate a team, to inspire a gift, to steer a vision, to establish Synergistic Rhythm, and so much more.

"Words are containers for power; you choose what
kind of power they carry." ~ Joyce Meyer

Questions To Consider

1. What are the positive gifts and talents on your team that can be inspired by your positive words?
2. What context is your world culture in your business? Positive or Negative? Inspiring or focused on what's not happening?
3. How are your internal email, text, and water cooler conversations? Are they feeding growth? Are they feeding Synergistic Rhythm?

Fuel Rhythm With Action

Janet not only recognized the gift in me but, after speaking directly to the heart of my talent, she opened doors for me. She took the initiative to guide me into processes and relationships that would nourish, energize, and nurture my gift for facilitation. I am forever grateful to Janet. Now, take a moment to reflect as a business leader: what next steps could you take to fuel the passions of your leaders? A very powerful key to fostering rhythm is to combine inspiring words with action. Intentional action demonstrates your commitment to your team.

> *"Raise your word, not your voice. It is rain that grows flowers, not thunder."* **~ Rumi**

Commitment Journal

An idea that feeds action with honor is creating a commitment list. Anytime as a leader you make a commitment, write it down, and then follow through. Actively doing this will nourish and feed a culture of honor and growth. When we purposely keep our commitments after we speak, text, or email, it will actually add a greater sense of stability, security, and team satisfaction.

Questions to Consider

1. What value would creating a commitment journal with action completed add to your culture?
2. How could you play a bigger role in leadership?

Word Power Builds or Destroys Culture

We have all experienced words that build up, as well as words that tear down. When we find ourselves weary or tired, casualness can lead to casualties. I am often asked, "How do we eliminate negativity and water cooler gossip?" It all starts with the leader and the leaders. Author Peter Daniels wrote a book titled *Mrs. Phillips, You Were Wrong.* His teacher had told him he would never amount to anything, yet Peter overcame those negative, destiny-altering words to become a very successful and wealthy businessman and philanthropist.

"Think twice before you speak, because your words and influence will plant the seed of either success or failure in the mind of another."
~ Napoleon Hill

The Cost of Speaking Your Mind

Consider the idea that every word we speak has the potential to build or tear down. Someone might say, "Well, I'm just going to speak my mind," but then I think that could be why their thoughts are so scattered. Before you speak, ask yourself if what you're about to say will add positive value. It's been suggested to give up your right to be right. We all know that a campfire goes out without wood. Now, imagine transforming your business culture simply by changing the type of words you use.

"Eating words has never given me indigestion."
~ Winston Churchill

"Japanese scientist Masaru Emoto performed some of the most fascinating experiments on the effect that words have on energy in the 1990's. When frozen, water that's free from all impurities will form beautiful ice crystals that look exactly like snowflakes under a microscope. Water that's polluted, or has additives like fluoride, will freeze without forming crystals. In his experiments, Emoto poured pure water into vials labeled with negative phrases like "I hate you" or "fear." After 24 hours, the water was frozen, and no longer crystallized under the microscope: It yielded gray, misshapen clumps instead of beautiful lace-like crystals. In contrast, Emoto placed labels that said

things like "I Love You," or "Peace" on vials of polluted water, and after 24 hours, they produced gleaming, perfectly hexagonal crystals. Emoto's experiments proved that energy generated by positive or negative words can actually change the physical structure of an object. The results of his experiments were detailed in a series of books beginning with The Hidden Messages in Water, where you can see the astounding before and after photos of these incredible water crystals."
~ Habib Sadeghi

Renaissance of Culture

Think of a house remodeling project: it may seem like things are getting worse due to demolition before they come alive with a fresh, new, updated design. Words can transform your world. A business leader has the ability to transform a business culture and rhythm by removing certain words and phrases from the vocabulary. Neurologists, psychologists, and wellness practitioners all have research on how the power of our words influences our mental and emotional state. Would you rather look at a rose garden all day or a garbage dump?

"Your gifts lie in the place where your values, passions and strengths meet. Discovering that place is the first step toward sculpting your masterpiece, Your Life." ~ Michelangelo

Trash the Trash

To begin the renaissance, consider eliminating phrases like "I am such a klutz" or "Every time I call clients, they never answer." Ask yourself why you might say, "Why does everyone pay late?" or "Why is sales always so difficult?" Here are a few more phrases to consider eliminating: "Here we go again, another new idea," or "Our team or company always has to do things over." Think for a moment about how cost-effective it would be to simply rephrase and replace the negative approach with a life-giving one. Research shows that words have power.

Questions To Consider

1. Take inventory of word phrases that are not building your business and people up.
2. How could you adjust your language to grow rhythm?
3. What edifying and honoring words can you speak into your team and business?
4. Does your approach put people in a box or invite them out of the box?

"If you don't design your own life plan, chances are you'll fall into someone else's plan. And guess what they have planned for you? Not much." ~Jim Rohn

The Influence of Time

Allow me to share a personal journey of building rhythm during my teenage years. I remember being 18 years old and buying a piece of land to build a house on, not knowing the road that lay ahead. I worked evenings and weekends to prepare for building this house before I turned 22. I recall working a full-time job framing houses for a construction company and then taking on many side jobs to earn extra cash to put toward this home.

The Good or The Great

I can remember being asked to do various things many times but choosing to stay focused on the vision at hand. It wasn't that I didn't want to do all sorts of things as a teenager; rather, my vision was larger and deeply rooted in my heart. I remember when the actual construction of the house began in October, with winter quickly approaching. The construction loan officer told me, "Ed, you have 140 days to finish this home with a certificate of occupancy."

"Number one reason people fail in life is because they listen to their friends, family, and neighbors." ~ Napoleon Hill

Power in Daily Consistency

I remember, at 21, starting my day at 6:30 a.m., working until 4:30 p.m., rushing to my grandparent's house to eat a meal, and then driving ten minutes to the house I was building. Even as winter set in, I continued day after day, for 130 straight days, to complete this house while working a full-time job. Many times, I found myself hitting a wall, feeling tired, lonely, and weary. But a greater vision and passion were fueling my heart's desire. The sacrifice at the time seemed so big, yet it was minor in the grand scheme of things. How is your team able to focus on enhancing Synergistic Rhythm?

"Singleness of purpose is one of the chief essentials for success in life, no matter what may be one's aim." ~ John Rockefeller

Opportunities in Adversity

It got dark at 5:30 over the winter, so I set up tall floodlights to keep working. When the house was complete, a neighbor came across the street and handed me a photo album documenting each day's progress. I was so grateful. They shared how they were moved by witnessing a young man's commitment and focus for almost four months.

The Heart Behind Sacrifice

Carrying a vision for your business, you will at times hit walls, become weary, hear criticism, and face financial challenges, but ask yourself what keeps you going through the day-to-day grind. For two years prior and one year afterward, I completed many projects for other people so that they would be available when I started building the house. I was so grateful for all who helped and supported the building of this home.

"The two most important days in your life are the day you are born and the day you find out why." ~ Mark Twain

Synergistic Rhythm Goes Beyond Logic

Building Synergistic Rhythm goes beyond the formulas; it has to be seated in a heart belief that you are doing something bigger than you. Adversity does pop its head up at times, but the vision field with passion will feed your heart to pivot around the potholes. During this time of building the home, many dynamics were going on in my life.

Key leadership principles I discovered building my first house.

Before I jump into a few key leadership principles that were valuable during this home-building experience, allow me to share my heart for a moment. Your vision that is authentically important to you will attract others to you. Being proactive and engaging your vision will awaken and reveal many gifts and talents within you and those who are there to help carry out your vision. There is this term I enjoy sharing with new entrepreneurs: If you get what you got, others will get what you got. We attract who we are.

I can remember those early mornings and late nights for almost 140 straight days, not only dealing with the elements of weather, fighting physical fatigue, and working a full-time job simultaneously. Many times, the hardest battle was the battle in my mind. At times, it was very lonely working towards completing this vision, and then, out of nowhere, a friend or family member would arrive to help. The consistency of daily habits was like railroad tracks through this entire process. Staying on those railroad tracks attracted more train cars to carry the payload. I want to encourage you that you and your team have so much untapped potential deep within.

Leadership Discovery

1. If you have a vision big enough and the passion to fuel it, no adversity is too big.
2. There is always a solution to create your way forward.
3. The power of showing up consistently.
4. The vision, purpose, and mission will feed and fuel daily habits.
5. Relational equity: having people that help carry the vision.
6. You can accomplish more than you think you can.
7. Time has a way of feeding the results.
8. This house inspired others with their dreams and goals.
9. Your gift will open up doors of favor.

"The difference between a successful person and others is not a lack of strength, not a lack of knowledge, but rather a lack of will."
~ Vince Lombardi

Being Fully Present

Allow me to introduce a very effective attitude to feed and grow Synergistic Rhythm. An attitude of "**being fully present**." Being fully present conveys that you matter and you're so important that everything else on the periphery is paused at that moment. It is an attitude of the heart that says, "When I am connecting with you, you have my full attention." Being fully present does not imply that there are no other important matters; rather, it communicates to the other person, "I am fully present with you." Being fully present adds tremendous value to a relationship and will nurture a synergistic rhythm in the connection. Being fully present is not a checklist item on a to-do list; it's a heartfelt value that emphasizes your presence matters.

"If you miss the present moment, you miss your appointment with life."
~ Thich Nhat Hanh

Surrender to The Moment

Think of a sponge soaking in water; it absorbs what it's immersed in. The sponge has to stay fully present to fully absorb. Surrendering to the moment does not mean ignoring the many tasks at hand. Think of it as taking a very deep breath, slowing down to nurture and feed the relationship in front of you. What value would it add for your teammate or customer if you and your team were truly present with them? What possibilities could arise from choosing to listen to understand and actually hearing them?

"Let me just pause a minute and drink in this moment. And if you film it, I'll be able to get free refills for life." ~ Jarod Kintz

Being fully present offers many benefits; one is that you can retain a wealth of details and information about others. They feel truly understood by you, and you can authentically remember what they are communicating. One practical way to develop this skill from a relaxed state is by asking genuinely curious questions about them. When they talk and we listen, the connection deepens.

> *"Give yourself a gift: the present moment."*
> *~ Marcus Aurelius*

Adding Value Being Present

Being fully present requires a willingness to engage with the now. To be in the moment requires a certain level of surrender to achieve full presence. Regardless of whether one is a people person, individuals of every personality type have the capacity to be fully present. Could it be that the value added by being present brings so much relational equity to your team or clients that the business thrives as a result? Imagine a business culture where people are eager to come to work because they feel genuinely valued! Consider how being fully present with someone adds value to your personal experience. People have an innate longing for authentic connections with others. While other businesses may offer similar products or services, the unique, authentic presence you and your team provide cannot be replicated. Encourage your team to discuss the value they derive from experiencing their teammates' full presence.

> *"When you make the present moment, instead of past and future, the focal point of your life, your ability to enjoy what you do and with it the quality of your life increases dramatically." ~ Eckhart Tolle*

Consider These Nuggets

1. How could you intentionally listen to understand?
2. How could you foster authentic team connection with no electronic devices? Practice face-to-face connection.

3. Consider starting the wave of being fully present by celebrating something your team has done well. Then, ask them what they are experiencing.

"I know people who are so immersed in road maps that they never see the countryside they pass through." ~ John Steinbeck

Benchmark For Rhythm

People will listen only to what they understand. Does your team grasp the concept of rhythm? Do they comprehend the significance of synergy, with its many components working together harmoniously? Can they identify it when it is present? The substantial assumption here is that everyone understands the concept of Synergistic Rhythm and its value to the team, customers, and company.

Pause for a moment and imagine standing at the edge of the ocean, yet no waves can be heard; it has become a lake, devoid of rhythm. Initially, we would be shocked. The ocean would lose part of its impact, its rhythmic sounds gone. The water is still there, but it is silent. Rhythm brings a multitude of sounds with it. When there is a positive rhythm, many recognize it, just as one knows the ocean for its constant waves.

"You need a pulse in a film. If I see a film that doesn't have rhythm, it's like listening to music that doesn't have rhythm; it doesn't really work." ~ Joe Wright."

Efficient Productivity with Rhythm

When you think of a sports team that taps into its rhythm or a movie that captures and grows within you, drawing you in—that's rhythm! Synergistic Rhythm is a producer's ability to create and orchestrate a movie by choosing the right cast, settings, language, and special effects to captivate viewers. It's the capacity of a producer, or a leader, to bring together many different parts to make a movie or a business culture so vibrant that time stands still and everyone is either eager to watch it again or looking forward to returning to the office the next day.

Consider what sets a great movie apart from a good one. A great movie must start with a great producer or leader. A great producer isn't necessarily one of the actors but possesses the ability to steer the rhythm of the entire movie until it's complete. This producer holds the heart's context and communicates daily with everyone involved.

"We don't make movies to make money. We make money to make more movies." ~ Walt Disney

Dealing With Distractions

How do you handle the constant opportunities that arise and threaten to derail your focus? Distractions can distort your purpose, blur your vision, and bring weariness to your mission. A very important key to staying on point is to recognize the difference between a mere distraction and an actual piece that completes the thousand-piece puzzle. Webster's definition of a distraction is "something that distracts: an object that directs one's attention away from something else."

What if distractions aren't personal but merely opportunities to respond with focus? A cyclist racing will see debris and steer around it, but their focus remains absolute, beyond the distraction. A motorcyclist at high speeds will always direct the bike toward the focus of their gaze. If their eyes are fixed on an obstacle, they will inevitably hit the obstacle.

"Distractions destroy action. If it's not moving you towards your purpose, leave it alone." ~ Jermaine Riley

Two Keys:

1. **Defining the Distraction:** The key is training your team on how to respond to them. Does the team know how to respond to distractions? Training is very important.

2. **Knowing The Main Attraction:** What is the main attraction of focus? Does the team know the next key or step? Think of it like a piece to the puzzle for that day, week, month, and so on.

Distractions Will Knock

"At times, the whole world seems to be in conspiracy to importune you with emphatic trifles. Friend, client, child, sickness, fear, want, charity, all knock at once at thy closet door and say,—'Come out unto us.' But keep thy state; come not into their confusion. The power men possess to annoy me I give them by a weak curiosity. No man can come near me but through my act." ~ Ralph Waldo Emerson

Knowing that distractions can be approached objectively—without emotional chaos—and with diligence, it's understood that there can be potholes on the road. Preplanning and training your team in situational awareness are essential. This preparation helps in effectively handling distractions while maintaining focus. Your daily business habits will be a major contributor to your ability to stay focused.

"Men stumble over pebbles, never over mountains."
~ H. Emilie Cady

What Meaning is Attached to Distractions

Think for a moment: Have you ever become emotional and taken a "no" personally during a sales call? Does that "no" mean you're not qualified, or that your product or service isn't awesome? It really depends on the meaning you attach to the "no." If you believe the "no" has greater value than your quality or service, that "no" can become a major distraction and wage mental battles with your confidence. The fact is, you're going to hear "no's." The more results you desire, the more "no's" you will hear. Think of it like mining for gold.

"Your results are the product of either personal focus or personal distractions. The choice is yours." ~ John Di Lemme

The meaning you attach to every "no" in business can be a game changer. Consider events such as not finding a parking space, encountering traffic jams, a computer breakdown, or a "no" in sales. These are all situations where we have a choice in our attitudes, responses, and the meanings we attach to them. There is great potential to shift the meaning of all events and situations in business. With systems, people, and culture, there will always be choices in our responses. We always have a choice in the meaning we attach. A decision can be made to respond in such a way that every event becomes a springboard for growing the business. Like every "no," setting the stage for a "yes." Think of it as drawing an arrow back in a bow.

"Refuse to attach a negative meaning to the word 'no.' View it as feedback. 'No' tells you to change your approach, create more value, or try again later." ~ Anthony Iannarino

Consider these responses:

1. "We can do this," instead of, "Why does this always happen?"
2. "We attract high-end clients everywhere we go," rather than, "Is there any business out there? The market is saturated."
3. "We have the best team and business synergy," as opposed to being an "EFF: Effective Fault Finder."

"Less distraction, more focus. Less gossip, more encouragement. Less past, more future. Less toxicity, more positivity." ~ Robin Sharma

Establish Efficiency and Effectiveness Indicators

Every ship captain relies on indicators and instruments to provide continuous feedback. In business, we must also have ways to receive feedback to measure efficiency and effectiveness. How can you create a hub for effective indicators that allow you to pivot back into rhythm? Think for a moment: Why do you do accounting? It goes far beyond the need to file taxes. Effective accounting is about measuring indicators to get feedback that can inform pivots, influencing the future in a positive way.

Before jets take off, there is a checklist. During the flight, constant indicators measure many aspects of the journey. After the jet lands, another checklist is used. It's impressive that a large jet can fly across the nation in five to six hours, both effectively and efficiently. The result of all these indicators is safety. Consider setting up indicators that foster a thriving rhythm and influence business growth.

"Efficiency is doing things right. Effectiveness is doing the right things."
~ Peter Drucker

Consider Establishing Indicators

1. Consider employee or subcontractor reviews every six months. Their feedback and your feedback can feed positive future growth.
2. Create a way to receive feedback consistently from your customers. Create a simple checklist list because people are busy. Consider rewarding their feedback.
3. Hire a really good bookkeeper to set up ways to measure all your numbers.
4. Think creatively about how to measure business intangibles like retention and dependability with your team, vendors, subcontractors, and even the types of customers.
5. Measure your marketing results and sales to become more effective.
6. Measure the effectiveness of your system. Consider asking constantly what is working and why. Ask what is not working and why not.
7. Measure the influence your culture has on growth. Meet with your team and ask for ways to improve and measure the culture. For example, if you establish a culture of celebration, you might notice that passion, synergy, and enthusiasm have consistently grown.
8. Listen to what people are saying and not saying. Create a simple daily way to do a shared document with accomplishments.

Rhythm Between Personalities

There are many combinations of personality temperaments; the goal is to learn how they all function and work synergistically together. Without delving too deeply into the major personality quadrants, the first step is to become aware of each temperament, its positive functions, and the ability to connect effectively. No personality type is better than another. Another thing to remember is that under pressure, each temperament can respond in a way that may not be as productive. I encourage you to at least take a personality test to understand both yourself and your team better. Developing a healthy rhythm within the team would be a powerful step toward growing your Synergistic Rhythm.

"There is nothing more attractive than a great positive personality. Its beauty never fades away with time." **Edmond Mbiaka**

CHAPTER TWELVE

Recognizing the "3 R's"

Recognizing the 3 R's

To develop and grow rhythm within your team and customers, recognizing the 3 R's can be a tremendous game changer and solution to feeding thriving growth. These three heart perspectives are great to be aware of when building teams. Avoiding them and allowing them to grow like weeds in a garden will be toxic. Think of them like a warning siren or a dashboard light going off.

Understanding and learning about the 3 R's can be great gold mines for growing healthy connections on your teams. Recognizing resentment right away can stop the escalator from going up to the second R resentment. The team's awareness and understanding can also be a powerful insight for cultivating relationships with your customers. If you've been a leader long enough, you most likely experienced the 3 R's at some point in relationships. The 3 R's, left unchecked or dealt with, will be very destructive to others and toxic for business rhythm. What are the 3 R's?

1. **Resentment**: This can be any type of negative emotion, frustration, jealousy, hatred, or envy towards another person.

2. **Resistance**: Is the cutting off, avoiding, or building a wall to protect and disconnect.

3. **Revenge**: Settling the score. To make a decision to attempt to get even or destroy another person.

Personal Responsibility

Before I elaborate on recognizing the 3 R's and pivoting from them, let's chat about a core belief of personal responsibility. The only person's heart and attitude we can only truly manage is our own. We get to choose our attitudes, mindsets, our choices, our actions. No one really has access to planting in the garden of our mind unless we give them permission consciously or subconsciously.

When talking about the 3 R's, think of coming from a context of personal responsibility. In other words, when I experience a certain attitude or behavior, I get to recognize it and choose my response, attitude, and actions. The freeing part is it removes the power of attitudes that try to plant in our minds. We can intentionally pivot into choosing Synergistic Rhythm. This is so freeing not to allow one person's attitude to disrupt or negatively affect your performance. Personal responsibility means that I get to make significant commitments or agreements. It also means that no matter what others decide, I choose to stay focused on the goal and vision.

"You must take personal responsibility. You cannot change the circumstances, the seasons, or the wind, but you can change yourself. That is something you have charge of." ~ Jim Rohn

Resentment

"The strong and painful bitterness you feel when someone does something wrong to you. It doesn't have actual physical weight, but it feels very heavy and can last a long time. Forgiveness is one way to get rid of resentment." ~ Vocabulary.com

"Our fatigue is often caused not by work, but by worry, frustration, and resentment." ~ Dale Carnegie

Have you ever been in a relationship where there was an unspoken expectation that you could feel? Uncommunicated expectations will foster judgments. In other words, something was expected to be done, but it was never communicated. This approach of avoidance can build resentment very quickly. Resentment is the seed that can lead to resistance and revenge if not redirected. For example, resentment can begin by repeatedly waiting in an express checkout line behind people with full carts in a lane designated for ten items or less. If this resentment begins to grow, the next checkout experience can be emotionally frustrating, leading to unwise choices.

"When you hold resentment toward another, you are bound to that person or condition by an emotional link that is stronger than steel. Forgiveness is the only way to dissolve that link and get free."
~ Catherine Ponder

Resistance

"A force that acts to stop the progress of something or make it slower."
~ Cambridge Dictionary

The second stage to be aware of is resistance. It could be a person, a customer, a sales call, or any team member whom you instinctively avoid engaging with immediately. Consider working in an environment where there is a teammate who is self-centered and receives all the accolades, fostering resistance. Imagine sitting in a chair with your arms locked out in front of you while another person stands in front of you, hand to hand, pushing. If you continue to resist without bending your elbows, the person sitting in the chair will tilt back and could fall to the floor. The solution is to bend the elbows and, in that moment, choose not to resist. Being aware of resistance is crucial before it escalates to revenge.

"Resistance is a result of our mind being attached to having things a certain way rather than the way they actually are. It is a mental habit of the ego that we need to become aware of in order to see the consequences. Only then can we see into our thought system and realize that nothing could be more of a waste of time than to resist and complain about what already is." ~ Lee L Jampolsky

Revenge

"An act or instance of retaliating in order to get even."
~ Merriam-Webster.com

Revenge is an intentional attempt to get even with someone. This can be a very dangerous place for me. One choice can have a very detrimental impact on a business. Simply put, if a customer or teammate has influenced a person to resist, it's likely to escalate to revenge.

"Before you embark on a journey of revenge, dig two graves."
~ Confucius

Let's say this has been building for some time, and a button is pushed, and you speak your mind. I know of a business owner who was on a difficult phone call with a customer, thought he hung up, and for four minutes or so went off about this customer to a coworker. Guess what? The customer heard the whole call! The customer called back and fired this business owner. Thousands of dollars in business lost for venting. The old saying goes, "Loose lips sink ships." Think before posting on social media or hitting send on electronic communications.

> *"You cannot get ahead while you are getting even."*
> *~ Dick Armey*

Establish a "20-minute rule." If you find yourself emotionally escalating from resentment to revenge and are on the verge of venting or giving that person a piece of your mind, wait twenty minutes. This pause may actually help you biologically to reframe your approach to the situation or relationship.

A Few Conflict Resolution Tips:

1. When the listener refrains from immediately responding with fixed solutions.
2. When they share, knowing they won't be shamed or punished.
3. Taking personal responsibility for our responses.
4. Consider the bigger picture before defending yourself.
5. Sometimes, the best answer is, "Thank you for sharing."
6. Discern what is actually at the root of the 3 R's in this situation.
7. Avoid debating and elevating yourself over the person expressing their concerns.

"If you want to be really successful, and I know you do, then you will have to give up blaming and complaining and take total responsibility for your life -- that means all your results, both your successes and your failures. That is the prerequisite for creating a life of success."
~ *Jack Canfield*

The Language of Business Rhythm

Business has a language of rhythm, just as music artists and dance have languages specific to their rhythms. Language is important because it shapes outcomes within its industry. For example, in sales, our language and words matter. Our tones, the order of our words, and the types of questions we ask can all influence the results.

"Language is a city to the building of which every human being brought a stone." ~ *Ralph Waldo Emerson*

Business carries many components, and taking the time to understand its language can be a profit changer. I mentioned earlier that people will really only listen when they understand. Many business leaders can have a tendency to avoid very important components of business growth due to not understanding the rhythm of accounting, cash flow, and conflict resolution. Let's explore a few types of business languages to understand.

"Words - so innocent and powerless as they are, as standing in a dictionary, how potent for good and evil they become in the hands of one who knows how to combine them." ~ *Nathaniel Hawthorne*

Castles Protect What's Valuable

Let's consider the image, familiar from history books, of a castle. Castles were built to protect what was valuable. They featured massive, high stone walls, moats, drawbridges, watchtowers, gatekeepers, and a series of inner chambers staffed by teams of people. What is so valuable that you need to protect it within your business, team, and destiny? How can you construct a castle-like system to safeguard your vision, focus, and thinking? A great first step is to take inventory of the thinking that has brought you this far. Then ask yourself, what kind of thinking or mindset will be necessary for you and your business to grow, scale, and set new records?

"Diversification is protection against ignorance. It makes little sense if you know what you are doing." ~ Warren Buffett

Building Reinforcements

To answer the question of what thinking or mindsets are necessary to elevate your business to the next level and break records, consider this: Have you ever noticed that castles have moats around them? Historians have written extensively about drawbridges, which are lowered only to allow into the castle what is desired. The moat served as a protective measure to keep potential invaders away from the castle walls. Negative thinking or pessimistic mindsets can be likened to those invaders. What could serve as your emotional moat? In other words, how can you ensure peace of mind, knowing that the moat provides your first line of defense? In business, your moat could consist of systems, processes, gatekeepers, secure access points, core values, and training.

"Interdependent people combine their own effort with the efforts of others to achieve their greatest success." ~ Stephen Covey

Lowering The Drawbridge

Lowering the drawbridge in business can symbolize various actions, such as hiring the right people, taking on suitable clients, and monitoring what you and your team read and listen to. Building a large castle represents a significant investment, undertaken because what it guards inside—often the destiny and future of a kingdom—is of utmost importance.

Typically, there would be a watchtower to survey who approaches the castle. Consider what constitutes your business's watchtower. Which early warning indicators provide feedback? What mechanisms could be implemented to offer real-time feedback? Envision a dashboard that monitors the rhythm of your business. Initially, one may start as a solo operation, but as the business expands, having personnel in your watchtower and operating the drawbridge is vital to protect your business's Synergistic Rhythm. A well-functioning drawbridge system is crucial. Entrusting your team with interconnected systems can foster growth beyond the confines of the "castle."

"Whatever we plant in our subconscious mind and nourish with repetition and emotion will one day become a reality.
~Earl Nightingale

The Gatekeeper

The castle has a gate to control who is allowed into the fortress. In ancient times, many bandits sought entry into castles with ill intent. What systems do you have in place to protect your mindsets, beliefs, and thinking? Who are your gatekeepers, and what training system is in place for them? Royalty relied on a team of gatekeepers to manage access so they could focus on the day's important tasks. Consider the qualities you seek in a gatekeeper. How can you safeguard your mental and emotional well-being with gatekeepers, systems, and culture? Gates serve as controlled access points; not everyone seeking entry was a friend to the castle dwellers. Similarly, not everyone who asks you questions has your best interests at heart. Thus, it's crucial to have gatekeepers who understand your business's ethos and are committed to protecting your time and resources, enabling you to remain focused on your core activities.

"When a gifted team dedicates itself to unselfish trust and combines instinct with boldness and effort, it's ready to climb. ~Pat Riley

The Gate

Castles feature multiple gates that provide access to various types of rooms. These gates can represent points of transition that lead to greater growth for your business. What are the gates in your business? For instance, sales, employees, customers, along with financial systems, can all be considered gates. What current gates present the most significant challenges to your business? View these adversities as opportunities to fortify the gate. Over time, some gates may simply need lubrication or repairs.

"Be willing to transition at every stage of your life. If your heart is open and you have an open mind, the blessing will flow." ~ T. D. Jakes

Gates Open Opportunity

Possibly, your business needs new gates of opportunity. What ideas lie deep in your heart, but you're unsure about how to act on them? What opportunities do you hear your team and clients talking about? Consider the power of the internet—it's a gate of opportunity with massive potential. By working with technology experts, you can have robots act as gatekeepers, protecting the computer's castle. How could you leverage the online world to gain greater access to even more gates? Like many industries, the online world is constantly changing. How could you prepare your business castle for the renaissance of all the new technologies? Amidst all the gates of opportunity, how can you steer the business's rhythm?

"Progress is impossible without change, and those who cannot change their minds cannot change anything." ~ George Bernard Shaw

Actions To Consider

1. How would you define your castle?
2. Who are your gatekeepers, and what are their roles? Do they understand their roles?
3. What are your business gates? What gates need some repairs or are completely closed up?
4. Who are those who operate the drawbridge, and what are their roles?

Threshing of Wheat

Growing up as a teenager working on an Amish farm, one of the greatest joys was bringing in the harvest. At the beginning of hot July, we would all look forward to threshing the wheat. We talked and prepared for it weeks in advance, cultivating such an expectation through our conversations about the wheat harvest. The preparation of equipment, roles of people, mules, and all the delicious food were essential. Despite the burning July heat, everyone knew they had a role to play and how important our focus was in gathering the wheat to be threshed. The assignments were established, and we all readily said yes.

"Teams make you better than you are, multiply your value, enable you to do what you do best, allow you to help others do their best, give you more time, provide you with companionship, help you fulfill the desires of your heart and compound your vision and effort." ~ John C. Maxwell

Definite of Purpose

Threshing is the process of separating the wheat kernels from the chaff. Oh, how the dust would fly during the shaking! We had a blast bringing full wagons of wheat shocks to the threshing area to be unloaded and then taking another wagon back out to the field. It was the shaking that removed the wheat kernels, which a conveyor then carried to a large storage bin. I remember loading the wagons all day long as the heat baked the fields. Despite the long, hot day of hard work, we would all be laughing and joking. There was a deep camaraderie and collaboration to bring in the harvest. There was truly Synergistic Rhythm, with everyone in their roles working together for a bigger vision. At the end of the day, we would climb up into the wheat bins and sit, mesmerized by all the wheat. Allow me to share a few keys I learned from threshing wheat to inspire Synergistic Rhythm.

"There is one quality which one must possess to win, and that is definiteness of purpose, the knowledge of what one wants, and a burning desire to possess it." ~ Napoleon Hill

Keys From Threshing

1. A definite collective purpose brought the harvest in without wavering.
2. Preparation in advance of the threshing supported our harvest rhythm
3. Every person was committed to their role.
4. The synergy was very positive, empowering, and energizing
5. Despite any adversity, we all stayed in solution, keeping our purpose on point.

6. Even with the heat of the day bearing down on us, we laughed and shared many fun stories. It seemed that the hotter it got, the more we had a blast, despite any obstacles.

Strength Training

An athlete works out, and the resistance from training strengthens their body and helps prevent injuries. The conflict with the opposing team sharpens the athlete, fostering growth and adjustment. The team vision—where every athlete performs their best to win championships—brings greater purpose to their physical, flexibility, and mental training. We have all heard stories of those who successfully completed Navy Seal training, a process that goes beyond the physical to forge mental and emotional strength. What training sharpens you, keeps you engaged, and grows your vision? Where is your vision leading you? What is one action you could take this week to begin strengthening your ability to realize your vision?

"When you do more than you're paid for, eventually you'll be paid for more than you do." ~ *Zig Ziglar*

Keeping Your Daily Edge

I remember asking a professional lawn care specialist, "How often do you sharpen the blades?" He responded quickly, "Once a day!"

I was thinking maybe once a month.

"I like my lawns looking great!" he said. He saw the vision of pristine lawns and understood how the sharpness of his blades contributed to that vision. He knew his secret sauce was very sharp blades. He shared that every day while cutting lawns around trees and shrubs, they'd encounter little surprises that dulled the blades. He had incorporated a 15-minute daily habit to maintain his cutting edge. What one daily fifteen-minute habit could transform your cutting edge? What is it costing your vision to work with a dull edge?

"A real decision is measured by the fact that you've taken a new action. If there's no action, you haven't truly decided." ~ Tony Robbins

Amish Frolic

A picture is often worth a thousand words. Allow me to share an image that exemplifies Synergistic Rhythm. As a teenager, I absolutely loved going to barn raisings, or "frolics," as we called them. These were gatherings of many from the local and regional Amish communities, coming together to work on a project for another farmer.

Such events would unfold with urgency, typically following a natural disaster, fire, or significant damage to a structure. Word would spread rapidly, and on the day, people would begin the cleanup to prepare for the new construction within days. I distinctly remember one frolic where we started in the morning with mostly just the floorboards laid out. Over 100 men and teenagers worked in harmony and unity to raise the entire shell by sunset. It is one thing to witness such an event from a distance but quite another, and a great gift to be a part of it—an experience that marks your life forever.

"Synergy – the bonus that is achieved when things work together harmoniously." ~ Mark Twain

I remember what seemed impossible: erecting a forty-foot wall that had been constructed on the ground. It was then raised with long poles as men began to climb up to attach braces. After two sections were set twenty feet apart, my friend and I started climbing up, securing braces as we went. It was as though everyone intuitively knew their role. I was overflowing with gratitude to be part of such a monumental project.

At 9:30, all the women and young ladies brought a veritable feast of food and drinks. Witnessing all the help, support, and kindness on display was a powerful moment.

The momentum only built as we approached lunch. Lunch itself was an extraordinary affair, feeding the multitude with more food than one could imagine. As a teenager, witnessing the collaboration was astonishing. Everyone seemed so joyful and vibrant, eager to assist and support this family in their time of need. All the provisions, the building materials, and the labor appeared as if by magic, summoned by the collective spirit of the community.

"Great things in business are never done by one person;
they're done by a team of people." ~ Steve Jobs

The afternoon and evening continued as people shared stories, laughed, and worked together diligently to get the entire building completely built. As the evening came and the sun began setting, it was truly remarkable to stand back and look at what was accomplished by so many people. All ages, both men and women, worked all day from the kitchen to the rooftops.

Rhythm Principles From Frolic

1. I never heard anyone complaining.
2. Like bees gathering honey, there was dynamic rhythm.
3. The fulfillment of what's possible in a short amount of time.
4. Collaborative hard work creates amazing results.
5. They volunteered their labor to serve one another.

"To build a strong team, you must see someone else's strength as a complement to your weakness and not a threat to your position or authority." ~ *Christine Caine*

CHAPTER THIRTEEN

Developing Thriving Ecosystems

The Rhythm in Nature

As we continue to solidify an organic rhythm for your business, let's explore a few discoveries from nature to create awareness for growing rhythm in your business. We did talk about the rhythm of nature in our early chapters. Have you ever noticed how nature seems to be in perfect rhythm? Have you noticed in nature that what is not growing is in decay? Have you observed the vibrancy of colors, textures, sounds, and fragrances? Which part of nature intrigues and captivates you?

Walking in Nature's Rhythm

Most days, I aim to be in nature early, amidst the quietness and stillness, attuned to its rhythmic voice. Nature has a beautiful rhythm. Have you ever noticed how birds begin chirping early in the morning, around the same time? It's nature's wake-up call, a symphony of rhythmic birdsongs. Getting out in nature early allows my heart to connect with that rhythmic voice, to write and reflect without the normal stresses and demands of the day. To develop a strong rhythm in your business, it will take intentionality and purpose, not from a place of stress or demand but by modeling nature's rhythm of peace and rest.

"The ocean asks for nothing, but those who stand by her shores gradually attune themselves to her rhythm." ~ Charles Dickens

Trees Stand Out

I've frequented a park for years, where I take reflective walks to write, inspire, and encourage. I've observed how the trees grow taller, and their branches extend to support more growth. I've also noticed the variety in their root systems. Some roots spread near the surface, while others delve deep underground. If we were to use trees as a metaphor for the growth of your leaders, it's clear that for the canopy of the tree to expand, the root system must also expand simultaneously.

"Fitting in is a short-term strategy that gets you nowhere. Standing out is a long-term strategy that takes guts and produces results."
~ Seth Godin

Marathon Mindset

One of the trees that I enjoy observing and often reference in training and speeches is the oak tree, which produces acorns. Research indicates that many oak trees begin producing acorns at around 30 years of age and cease production after 80 years. In the business world, people can become frustrated when they don't see immediate results. An oak tree endures many storms and seasons before yielding its first acorn. This suggests that, although a business might generate a substantial profit in its first year, it's beneficial to adopt a long-term, marathon mindset rather than a sprint mindset.

"If you can build a muscle, you can build a mindset.
~ Jay Shetty

Exponential Results

One oak tree that stays healthy and thriving surrounded by nature's rhythm produces, according to different researchers, approximately 10 million acorns. Think for a moment about the ecosystem that one oak tree contributes to nature's rhythm. Again, using an oak tree as a metaphor for a thriving leader. To develop a leader takes time; there is art and science to leadership. But, leadership can be taught with a willing leader. What is possible through one thriving leader who embraces a thriving growth rhythm day after day, week after week, month after month, year after year? How can one idea feed your business rhythm, developing exponential results?

"The results you achieve will be in direct proportion to the effort you apply." ~ Denis Waitley

Your Business Potential

Your business and life possess tremendous potential. Consider for a moment the oak trees waiting to emerge from within the acorns. Reflect on the potential that lies deep within the nature of that seed.

The stewardship of the acorn will determine the future of the forest ecosystem, air quality, food supply, furniture availability, and whatever else one's imagination can conceive. Envision your business systems, people, and culture as acorns brimming with potential.

How these seeds are planted and nurtured in the hearts of your people will determine the extent of growth or lack thereof. For acorns to grow, they must be planted in soil. Sometimes, acorns face potential destruction by a squirrel's hunger, and other times, they are carried off to be planted elsewhere.

What if that adversity is actually the squirrel carrying your future growth? Consider your business as the greatest opportunity to plant acorns with every interaction, transaction, and relational moment. What's possible within the treasury of your business day? Plant seeds!

"Everything we do seeds the future. No action is an empty one."
~ Joan D. Chittister

A Thriving Ecosystem

Consider for a moment how your business influences your local economic ecosystem. What if a thriving business could elevate your local region into a thriving ecosystem? Envision the possibilities within a forest of oak trees—how businesses interconnect at the root level, supporting each other to create a dynamic, living community ecosystem. Whether indirectly or directly, your business has the potential to bring long-term, thriving health to your town or city, akin to the enduring strength of an oak tree.

Healthy Ecosystems Cause Growth

Have you ever sat under a large oak tree on a hot, sunny day? The experience of the coolness of the shade acts as a refuge for people and animals alike. Similarly, when homes are built, trees are often strategically placed to provide protection against the hot elements and the winter's north winds. In business, healthy, thriving leaders can provide high levels of insight, inspiration, and impact during the various seasons a community experiences. Since your business is an ecosystem within another ecosystem, consider taking a moment to ponder the contributions your business makes to the interconnected ecosystems of which you are a part.

"Unless you try to do something beyond what you have already mastered, you will never grow." ~ Ralph Waldo Emerson

Your Influence and Impact

When you ponder the massive amounts of acorns produced from 50 years of solid acorn production, think for a moment about the ecosystem that supports it. From animals carrying and planting acorns all over the area, to the food source it supplies, to the potential new oak trees that add value to our air quality, the ability to make furniture, and build homes. What acorns does your business produce? How are your business acorns influencing your local economy, livelihoods, and community?

Multiplying Factor

If an oak tree produces an average of 10 million acorns, one has to wonder how many oak trees are produced from one tree over 50 years. How could you pivot, adapt, and adjust what your business produces to create a multiplying factor not only in your business and life but also in the community around you? Think about the economics for a moment: when there is a thriving business, it lessens the burden on the community around it. What is your business's X factor? What sets your business apart from others?

Each business owner has a unique, and oftentimes different, reason that they get up and go daily. With a multiplying mindset, what is it that gets you up daily to nurture your leaders, investing in your leaders to produce long-lasting oak trees? When you walk into a home, notice the oak furniture, potential kitchen cabinets, and outdoor lawn furniture. They all started with an acorn, or seeds, so to speak. I want to encourage you to continue to feed the roots of your vision, your purpose, and mission.

Developing Synergistic Rhythm will allow you to do multiple things simultaneously, the natural way, so to speak, from a place of peace and rest.

"Working together precedes winning together...collaboration is multiplication." ~ John C. Maxwell

Questions to Consider

1. What are your business reproducing acorns?
2. Who in your business are your oak trees?
3. How can you feed the root of your business ecosystem?
4. What nutrition feeds the life of your business ecosystem?
5. What oak trees are you reproducing long-term through your business?

Power of: "AS ONE!"

In the movie *Gladiator*, they faced overwhelming odds. Men were placed in an arena as though they were thrown into a pool of sharks or a lion's den. In this exhilarating and inspirational moment, one of the men, Maximus, stood up and declared, "If we stick together 'AS ONE,' we will survive! If we try to defeat the enemy individually, we will all die." The movie has a way of drawing you in and inspiring many business and life moments.

Standing out in the open arena, they didn't know what would come out of the gates of terror. But they made a choice to stand with great bravery and courage, unified "as one," to face the chariots and horsemen with blades of death. As a chariot charged directly towards them, they would shout "AS ONE!" and lock their shields together, digging them into the dirt. The chariots would be launched over the top of them, dismantling and disabling the chariot of death. Maximus led the men to victory, regaining their freedom from a tyrant, brutal ruler. This moment was a snapshot of two profound rallying words—"AS ONE!"

A Confident Conviction

Within your business systems, people, and culture, is there a situation that seems a bit overwhelming? What golden possibilities could arise by inspiring those around you to come up with a dynamic solution? How could you inspire your leaders and have a rallying cry like "AS ONE"? What would it look like to join shields together, overcoming the situation and flipping the switch? In *Gladiator,* it only took one man with tremendous conviction to win the hearts of the warriors and the people. His confident conviction infused collective bravery into all the other warriors. Leadership requires looking beyond the obstacles and situations, rallying others with "AS ONE!" Leadership is influence.

"A true leader has the confidence to stand alone, the courage to make tough decisions, and the compassion to listen to the needs of others."
~ Douglas MacArthur

Questions To Consider

1. What does one look like?
2. What are your business shields?
3. Who are your leaders that would lock shields?
4. What would be the return on the investment of time growing through the situation?

Facing All Odds

I met a distinguished man named Morris E. Goodman. He was in our area to speak many years ago, and I noticed that his neck was a little stiff. Instinctively, I felt something must have happened on his journey. While driving to the venue where he was speaking, he would pull out a notepad and jot things down. Curious, I asked him, "Mr. Goodman, I noticed you frequently refer to your notepad. Is there anything we can do for you?"

He replied, "I get many ideas; some are million-dollar ideas. I trust the paper more than my mind."

The key principle he demonstrated was his teachable spirit in capturing ideas that would come almost instantly; he would not take any idea for granted. He mentioned that many ideas connect to others. As a business leader, this serves as a great reminder of the importance of being aware of ideas, listening, and even developing a list of ideas.

Power of One Question

During our car ride, he began to share his journey as a business owner selling insurance. He recounted how his small plane had hit a power line and how he had faced a near-death experience. I was intrigued by his attitude, mindset, and conviction, which led me to ask more questions. A principle to keep in mind when you're with other leaders is to have three to five questions ready to ask them. Like an engine warming up after being started, he was sharing his entire nine-month journey of miracles. He talked not only about his journey but also about many business and leadership principles. Being intentional around greatness and cultivating that greatness is actually our responsibility. Great leaders love to share when they are asked.

"The best scientists and explorers have the attributes of kids! They ask questions and have a sense of wonder. They have curiosity. 'Who, what, where, why, when, and how!' They never stop asking questions, and I never stop asking questions, just like a five-year-old." ~Sylvia Earle

S.N.I.O.P.

I may not recall every single detail perfectly, but the essence of what he shared with me that day profoundly influenced my life. Allow me to share a few nuggets from our conversation. He emphasized the power of expectation—a clear, definite purpose. He referred to it as S.N.I.O.P., which stood for "Susceptible to the Negative Influence of Other People." He elaborated, mentioning that his daughter had placed those letters on his nightstand as a reminder. His established connection with her ensured that not a single person could speak negatively about his future health prognosis. When he was going into trauma surgery, he had a one-in-a-thousand chance of surviving the neck surgery that would fuse his spine back together. Hearing the list of things he faced—being unable to walk, speak, or move and being paralyzed—was overwhelming for me.

"How we think not only affects our own spirit, soul, and body but also people around us." ~ Dr. Caroline Leaf

Power of Expectation

His nickname is "The Miracle Man." After personally chatting with him, I realized his perspective and attitude were next-level, different from anyone I've ever met. He set a goal after his first surgery to walk out of the hospital by the end of the year, despite the doctor saying he would never walk again. He stared directly at his prognosis and began to think, speak, and create a mindset through faith that he was going to walk out of the hospital. He underwent nearly 20 surgeries, and the hospital's doctors were remarkable in their surgical skills.

> *"You can do and have and be things that people once said that's impossible for you to do and have and be."*
> *~ Morris E. Goodman*

Mental Movie

Morris Goodman's part was his mental movie—playing the right mental movie all day, every day. He carried an expectation that began to manifest, first with his lungs coming back, then his ability to speak again. Going through therapy to learn to walk again was truly inspiring. Every step of the way was filled with suffering, defeat, pain, and loss, but he stayed the course. He kept focused on the ultimate result, which for him was not only speaking but physically walking out of the hospital.

> *"Man becomes what he thinks about."*
> *~ Morris E. Goodman*

Going Through the Goal

Many times, the danger is actually hitting the goal. He taught me that the goal is only a step and that we must see beyond the goal. The goal is a step, a part of a bigger dream and vision. As we were getting closer to the speaking engagement, I was curious about him hitting his goal of walking out of the hospital. After the longest marathon of survival, rehabilitation, and focus, on the day he was exiting the hospital, he asked them to stop the wheelchair before he crossed the door threshold. They said, "Mr. Goodman, it's against hospital policy. We have to wheel you out."

He said, "If I don't walk out of this hospital, I will not achieve my goal."

Keep in mind they said he would be paralyzed for all his life. He had a goal that was beyond all natural possibilities. He convinced them to stop; he stood up, fell down, and then, one of the times he stood up, he slid his legs and hobbled across the threshold. He sat down with the biggest smile and said, "I have achieved this goal, but I am focused on greater goals."

Hearing that, I was in tears with streams running down my face, as I had many flashes of different events in my own personal life.

"There's a difference between interest and commitment. When you're interested in doing something, you do it only when it's convenient. When you're committed to something, you accept no excuses; only results." ~ Kenneth Blanchard

Commitment to Goals

I was sitting in the backseat, thinking, *Gosh, how many times have I not completed a goal because of a distraction?* I realized I was sitting with a man who was already looking beyond the goal. That day was a life-changing moment for me. He went on to build a philanthropic organization and became an inspirational speaker, helping others overcome impossibilities.

One of the biggest lessons I learned from him was that he simply did not think like anyone I had ever met. Adversity was a launchpad for him; he saw challenges as great opportunities. His relentless focus and commitment to a goal taught me a powerful lesson in persistence that day. He would say, "All things are possible to him who believes." A powerful nugget I learned about business that day was how "consistent persistence" is absolutely instrumental in achieving anything great.

"Motivation is what gets you started. Commitment is what keeps you going." ~ Jim Rohn

Nuggets Learned from Mr. Goodman

1. Write every idea and important thought down.
2. Play the right mental movie all day, every day.
3. A goal is a step to a dream. Never stop at the goal, but always have another goal.
4. S.N.I.O.P.—Many look at the natural prognosis; he saw the promise of health. So, he knew his belief system was susceptible to the negative influence of other people.
5. He took his tragic impact and turned it into influential inspiration.
6. His heart of benevolence was at the root of all he did.

Principles From 20,000 Square-Foot Home

I remember receiving a call to solve a crown molding challenge for a potential client almost two hours away. Have you ever received a call where you needed to ask a few more questions to ensure it was a good investment of time? I felt really good about the connection during the call, so we scheduled to drive out with tools and a vehicle to address the challenge. The house, already constructed, resembled an estate from a movie when we pulled up to the front elevation. The front door was massive, and the homeowner greeted us with joy and hospitality. The room we were to work in was larger than my first house. The three carpenters I brought along were a bit nervous, especially since the client asked to sit and watch us the entire time. After some conversation, we spent an extraordinary and successful few hours there.

How We Answer Questions

The homeowner asked, "What else can you do?"

I responded, "What else would you like to have done?"

He then said, "Let me show you this exquisite library I want built."

He opened the 21-light solid mahogany doors, leading to the most beautiful display of ornamental trim work. He inquired if we could complete it by a certain date. I committed that four of us would have it finished within the timeframe. I knew that by taking on this particular project, I would open up tremendous opportunities with this client. Often, it's not only the skill we use to complete a task but also the culture, context, and consistency with which we perform it. The clients were some of the most extraordinary, kind, and benevolent people you could ever work with, demonstrating a tremendous capacity for excellence.

Setting The Stage

After the library was completed, he expressed his gratitude for all that had been accomplished. He suggested, "Going forward, let's make an agreement: I will pay you cost-plus for everything and write out a check every month." We worked at the house four days a week for three years and three months. I realized quite quickly that we are often being interviewed for future opportunities. How can your awareness of your customers feed into your future business rhythm?

Accommodate, Adapt, and Adjust

He would fly his airplane to our area just to make material selections, even if it was for a single type of Italian marble for his 12,500-bottle wine cellar, making a round-trip flight. Because of our open communication and willingness to go the extra mile, we built a high level of mutual trust. Every craftsman brought onto the job was briefed about the culture. As we discussed earlier in this book, systems, people, and culture were imperative and very important to this homeowner, especially for this project.

Culture Communication

They were the type of people who demanded absolute excellence and wanted things done their way, so we decided to accommodate their heart's desire. This required looking ahead with each of our craftsmen, suppliers, and subcontractors to ensure they understood our expectations and the culture specific to this project. Everyone grasped that the bigger picture of this project was dynamic Synergistic Rhythm. As a result, we were all able to work on a 20-bedroom home that was a once-in-a-lifetime type of project.

Principles to Carry Synergistic Rhythm: We Learned Working on This Estate to Feed and Fuel Business Growth!

1. The power of asking questions to chisel away at anything that could bring uncertainty or confusion
2. Listening to understand what was their expectation.
3. The importance of caring culture for three years and three months.
4. Treat every phone call like the Super Bowl.
5. Your team and people will rise to your inspiring leadership capacity.
6. It's OK to express areas that you need to do more research on with your clients. They always appreciate the candor.
7. Holding Context and Culture is an Intentional.
8. Your team and people will rise to the level of expectation that you carry.
9. The importance of a caring and abundant mindset.
10. Treat every person on your team as the most valuable player.

Call To Action

In the context of taking action, consider for a moment what the main keys from this book spoke to you. What three specific action steps could you apply right now? Questions are keys that can unlock your potential; what continued action plan could you establish over the next month, quarter, and year? Consider keeping this book as a business handbook, referring to it, and even walking through it with your team. I invite you to create your way to a better day — you've got what it takes! How can you begin today to establish a rhythm with your systems, people, culture, and core values?

This book can be an invaluable business resource for your team and new hires. Consider having your entire leadership team go through this book together to foster discussion and discovery. It was the greatest honor to share some insights on Synergistic Rhythm with you in this book.

THANK YOU FOR READING MY BOOK!

I hope that this book has inspired you and that you have found your *Rhythm*. Just to say thanks for buying and reading my book, I would like to give you some free resources!

Scan the QR Code Here:

I appreciate your interest in my book and value your feedback as it helps me improve future versions of this book. I would appreciate it if you could leave your invaluable review on Amazon.com with your feedback. Thank you!

Made in the USA
Middletown, DE
15 March 2024

50877578R00119